The Canadian Spelling Program 2.1

7

Ruth Scott
Jeff Siamon

0612

gagelearning

© 1998 Gage Learning Corporation
1120 Birchmount Road
Toronto, Ontario M1K 5G4
1-800-668-0671
www.nelson.com

We acknowledge the financial support of the Government of Canada through the Book Publishing Industry Development Program for our publishing activities.

We acknowledge the Government of Ontario through the Ontario Media Development Corporation's Ontario Book Initiative.

National Library of Canada Cataloguing in Publication Data
Main entry under title:

Scott, Ruth, 1949-
The Canadian spelling program 2.1, 7

ISBN 0-7715-1595-2

1. Spellers. I. Siamon, Jeff. II. Title.

PE1145.2.S394 1998   428.1   C97-930907-7

Review

The authors and publisher gratefully acknowledge the contributions of the following educators to *The Canadian Spelling Program 2.1*:

Gerry Brennan
Kimberley, BC

Robert T. Dawe
St. John's, Newfoundland

Irene Heffel
Edmonton, Alberta

Eleanor McLaughlin
Fredericton, New Brunswick

Sharon Morris
Etobicoke, Ontario

Lynette Owoc
Brampton, Ontario

Acknowledgments

Every reasonable effort has been made to trace ownership of copyrighted material. Information that would enable the publisher to correct any reference or credit in future editions would be appreciated. **Cover** (Skater) David Vincent / Tony Stone Images / **p. 7** Joyce Barkhouse, *Pit Pony*. (Toronto: Jeanpac Series, Gage Educational Publishing, 1990), 20. / **p. 12** Jean Little, "The Training of Zephyr." Appeared in *Friends for Life*. (Scarborough: Nelson Canada, 1993), 24. / **p. 16** Max Braithwaite, *Whooping Crane Adventure*. (Toronto: Gage Educational Publishing Company, 1988), 179. / "The Thesaurus Regatta" by Wiley © 1996, Washington Post Writers Group. Reprinted with permission. / **p. 19** Animal Crackers cartoon reprinted with permission—Toronto Star Syndicate. Copyright: 1996 Tribune Media Services. / **p. 20** Susan Forest, *The Dragon Prince*. (Toronto: Jeanpac Series, Gage Educational Publishing, 1990), 79. / **p. 30** Martyn Godfrey, *Mystery in the Frozen Lands*. (Toronto: James Lorimer & Company, Publishers, 1988), 28. / **p. 33** ZIGGY © 1984 ZIGGY AND FRIENDS INC. Dist. By UNIVERSAL PRESS SYNDICATE. Reprinted with permission. All rights reserved. / **p. 37** Nazneen Sadiq, *Heartbreak High*. (Toronto: James Lorimer & Company, Publishers, 1988), 47. / **p. 38** B.C. cartoon by permission of Johnny Hart and Creators Syndicate Inc. / **p. 40** B.C. cartoon by permission of Johnny Hart and Creators Syndicate Inc. / **p. 46** Grace Richardson, *Into That Darkness Peering*. (Toronto: Jeanpac Series, Gage Educational Publishing, 1989), 15. / **p. 53** ADAM © 1995 UNIVERSAL PRESS SYNDICATE. Reprinted with permission. All rights reserved. / **p. 56** Roch Carrier, "The Hockey Sweater." Translated by Sheila Fischman. Appeared in *Laugh Lines*. James Barry, Glen Huser, and Sharon Siamon, eds. (Scarborough: Nelson Canada, 1993), 35. / **p. 60** Robert Mason Lee, *Death and Deliverance*. (Toronto: Macfarlane Walter & Ross, 1992), 145. / **p. 64** Susan Forest, *The Dragon Prince*. (Toronto: Jeanpac Series, Gage Educational Publishing, 1990), 103. / **p. 66** CALVIN AND HOBBES © 1989 Watterson. Reprinted with permission of UNIVERSAL PRESS SYNDICATE. All rights reserved. / **p. 68** Sharon Siamon, *Ski For Your Mountain*. (Toronto: Jeanpac Series, Gage Educational Publishing, 1983), 160. / **p. 72** Andrew Revkin, "A Car With a Mind of Its Own." Appeared in *Viewpoints*. Christine McClymont, ed. (Scarborough: Nelson Canada, 1990), 127. / **p. 90** FOR BETTER OR FOR WORSE © 1993 Lynn Johnston Prod., Inc. Reprinted with permission of UNIVERSAL PRESS SYNDICATE. All rights reserved. / **p. 93** Jean Mills, *Wild Dog Summer*. (Scarborough: Nelson Canada, 1990), 48. / **p. 112** Sylvia McNicoll, *Blueberries and Whipped Cream*. (Toronto: Jeanpac Series, Gage Educational Publishing, 1989), 71. / **p. 114** CHARLIE cartoon reprinted with permission—Toronto Star Syndicate. Copyright: 1996 Tribune Media Services. / **p. 119** CALVIN AND HOBBES © 1992 Watterson. Reprinted with permission of UNIVERSAL PRESS SYNDICATE. All rights reserved. / **p. 120** Max Braithwaite, *The Muffled Man*. (Scarborough: Nelson Canada, 1989), 120. /

Editor: Evelyn Maksimovich
Cover and Text Design: Pronk&Associates
Illustration: Pronk&Associates, Steve Attoe
Photography: Ron Tanaka

ISBN 0-7715-**1595-2**
4 5 TCP 06 05
Written, printed, and bound in Canada.

Contents

To the Student

Why study spelling?

You may wonder why you are still studying spelling. After all, with computer spell checks who needs to study spelling? And besides, aren't the ideas more important than the spelling?

Let's take these questions one at a time.

What about spell checks?

True, spell checks are a wonderful tool, but they are no substitute for your own spelling knowledge. The reason: spell checks can *spell*, but they can't *read*. A spell-checking program will miss errors made with homophones (*there/their/they're*) and easily confused words (*sit/set*) every time. As long as the word is spelled correctly, the spell checker doesn't care whether or not the word makes sense. That's your job.

Is spelling important?

No, not if you never read or write. But that's unlikely. Daily, you are bombarded with forms of communication that rely on your ability to spell: magazine articles, comic strips, notes to friends, shopping lists, billboards, contest entry forms, e-mail messages, product labels, greeting cards, school assignments.

Imagine, for a moment, that you want to surf the Net for information about skateboarding. Key *s-c-a-t-e-b-o-r-e-d-i-n-g* into your search engine and you'll get a message that reads something like, "No documents match the query. You may want to check the spelling." If you don't at least know how to spell the base word *skate*, not even a dictionary will be able to help you.

Research shows that spelling, unlike riding a bicycle, is not a skill that is learned once and never forgotten. It takes time and practice to become a good speller. The English language is filled with words that are exceptions to rules, contain silent letters, and have strange pronunciations. Sometimes, sounding out a word is no help at all.

Is spelling important? You be the judge.

Short Vowels

Telephone Message

Date: _May 16_ Time: _1:45 p.m._
For: _Jarita_
From: _Mr. Rawal_
Phone #: _111 - 1234_

Please call	✓	Urgent!	
Will call back		No response necessary	✓

Message: _Wants to know if you're available for baby-sitting after lunch on Saturday. Needs someone to watch baby during Kevin's birthday party. Let him know before seven. P.S. If you can't make it, I'll go insted ...I need the money!_

Every syllable in a word contains a vowel. Short vowels make the sounds /a/ as in <u>back</u>, /e/ as in <u>speck</u>, /i/ as in <u>chin</u>, /o/ as in <u>pond</u>, and /u/ as in <u>mud</u>. Sometimes spelling problems happen when there is more than one way to create a short vowel sound in writing.

Did you notice the spelling of the word <u>instead</u> in the phone message? The writer was probably thinking of the most common way of creating the sound /e/ as in <u>red</u>.

basketball
cassette
crackle
difficult
exhibit
graph
helicopter
husky
nonsense
profit
rocky
Saskatchewan
September
static
swiftly

OTHER PATTERNS

guest
*guide
limb
rhythm
*through

Thinking about Words

1. The underlined letters in this list of words taken from the phone message are all short vowels. Sort the words under these five headings: /a/ as in <u>bat</u>; /e/ as in <u>let</u>; /i/ as in <u>clip</u>; /o/ as in <u>sock</u>; /u/ as in <u>sunny</u>. Remember, think about the *sound* that you hear, not just the spelling!

w<u>a</u>nts	b<u>a</u>by-sitting	som<u>e</u>one	S<u>a</u>turday	<u>a</u>fter	K<u>e</u>vin
w<u>a</u>tch	<u>o</u>n	<u>i</u>f	l<u>u</u>nch	s<u>e</u>ven	l<u>e</u>t

2. Write a topic on a piece of paper and exchange it with a partner. Challenge your partner to list at least ten words containing a short vowel sound that relate to the topic. For example, the topic "television" might include words such as *ch<u>a</u>nnel, v<u>o</u>lume, s<u>i</u>tcom, dr<u>a</u>ma, <u>e</u>ntertainment,* and so on. Use a dictionary to check each other's work.

Word Pattern

The short vowel sound /a/ is usually spelled with the letter **a**; /e/ with **e**; /i/ with **i**; /o/ with **o**; /u/ with **u**.

Working with Words

1. Complete these sentences by supplying a short vowel for each blank.

   a) The h_lic_pter made a d_ffic_lt l_nding on the r_cky slope because there was a crack in one of _ts blades.

   b) Our Science Fair _xh_bit on st_tic el_ctr_city _ncluded gr_phs and a cass_tte th_t explained our exp_rim_nt.

   c) L_st S_pt_mber, the b_sketb_ll team tr_velled to S_sk_tchewan on the pr_fits they made from s_lling m_gazines.

2. The words **basketball** and **helicopter** are examples of new words that have been formed to describe inventions in sports and technology. The first is a compound word formed logically from the two words *basket* and *ball*. The second takes its meaning from the French word *helicoptere*, which has two Greek roots: *heliko* meaning "spiral" + *pteron* meaning "wing."

   Combine word parts from each of the two columns to create terms from the worlds of sports and technology.

Sports		Technology	
bob	cycling	micro	board
acro	ball	down	word
bi	diving	cyber	commuting
hand	lifting	joy	media
racket	sledding	key	load
moto	batics	multi	out
steeple	cross	pass	space
sky	chase	tele	chip
weight	ball	print	stick

3. The words **guest** and **guide** contain the sound /g/ spelled **gu**. Complete this list of words containing the **gu** spelling pattern:

   a) opposite of innocent   gu_ _ _ _

   b) to fight with words   _ _gu_

   c) stringed instrument   gu_ _ _ _

   d) invited visitor   gu_ _ _

   e) conceal identity   _ _ _gu_ _ _

   f) unsure of answer   gu_ _ _

4. Sometimes remembering the shape of a word will help you to recall silent letters or other details. Link each of these shapes to a list word:

1. Can you figure out these phone messages? Rewrite each message as a complete sentence.

    a) No xtra seats aval. Meet btwn gates 7&8 @ 4 p.m. C U B4 the game.

    b) From: Gene. Time: 11:04 a.m.
        Message: Call. Evenings. Project <u>NOT</u>! cancelled. 456-1234.

    c) Ms. Rinaldi. After 10. Train. Pls leave key. Don't W8 up.

2. The short vowel sound /e/ in <u>instead</u> is an unusual short-vowel pattern. Solve each of these clues by finding a word that has the same sound pattern as *instead*. Use each of the words in a sentence.

    a) grooves on a tire

    b) heavy metal that protects against x-rays

    c) uppermost part of your body

    d) opposite of alive

    e) best way to hold a ladder

LANGUAGE MATTERS

Etymology is the study of words and their origins. Many of the most common words in English have their origins in other languages. The word <u>telephone</u>, for example, comes from the Greek word *tele* meaning "far," and *phone* meaning "sound." Literally translated, *telephone* means "sound from far."

Can you list ten other *tele* words and their meanings?

3. Work with a partner to role-play a telephone conversation in which the person answering the phone must write down a message from the caller. The caller should try to include several list words in his or her message. Exchange the written message with other groups. Can they understand the message? Are the list words spelled correctly?

4. Using either art supplies or a computer software program, design a form on which to write phone messages (see p. 1 for an example). Glue or staple copies of your forms together and use them at home.

The Editing Desk

Parts of Speech Every word you use can be classified into one of eight or more parts of speech. Here are four of them:

Noun: a word that names a person, place, or thing

Verb: a word that shows action or the fact that something exists

Adjective: a word that tells more about a noun or pronoun

Adverb: a word that tells more about a verb (and sometimes an adjective or other adverb)

1. Match as many list words as you can to each of the parts of speech listed above. For example, **graph** describes a mathematical diagram (noun) and indicates the action of drawing a graph (verb).

2. Choose a paragraph from one of your written assignments. Circle all the nouns, verbs, adjectives, and adverbs in your paragraph. Write the part of speech above each circle.

3. Complete each sentence by selecting a list word that matches the part of speech indicated.

  a) The rescue team jumped out of the _____ as it landed on the _____ ground. (noun, adjective)

  b) The date was the fifth of _____. (noun)

  c) The rescuers had to move _____ over a frozen river to reach the crash site. (adverb)

  d) As they ran, the ice began to _____ and then break under their feet. (verb)

  e) They realized that they were in a _____ situation. (adjective)

  f) Suddenly, they heard a _____ voice cry out. (adjective)

LANGUAGE MATTERS

New words are added to the English language all the time. Here are some words followed by the dates when they were first noted in English. Do you know what events or trends might have resulted in the widespread use of these words?

atom	(1801)	automation	(1948)	gravity	(1642)
microwave	(1931)	discothèque	(1951)	vitamin	(1905)
[to] audition	(1935)	teenager	(1930)	mini	(1961)

2 Long Vowels
vowel-consonant-e

These notes contain many samples of long vowels. Long vowels say their own names and there are several ways to create the long vowel sound in writing. One common way is with the vowel-consonant-e pattern, as in <u>cake</u>, <u>hope</u>, <u>scene</u>, <u>time</u>, and <u>dune</u>.

Snowshoe Hares
- found in the Canadian Rockies
- white with black-tipped ears
- twilight best time to see them
- males called "bucks," females called "does"
- survival rate only 10-50%
- makes home under spruce branches, dense brush, etc.
- gestation period complete in 37 days

advice
awaken
Chinese
choke
dilute
excitement
operate
polite
realize
refuse
sincere
sore
sphere
volume
whole

OTHER PATTERNS
*always
bisect
*everyone
semifinal
universe

Thinking about Words

1. The following words, taken from the jot notes, contain a long **i** sound. Rewrite those words that form the long vowel sound / ī / with the i-consonant-e pattern. Then come up with two more words that follow the same pattern and add them to the list.

| white | twilight | time |

2. Rewrite those words from the list below that use the a-consonant-e pattern to create the long vowel sound /ā/.

| male | failure | makes |
| rainy | rate | female |

3. Reread the jot notes on snowshoe hares to find examples of the unit pattern for long **o**, **u**, and **e**.

Word Pattern

Long vowel sounds are commonly created with the vowel-consonant-e pattern, as in <u>case</u>, <u>tune</u>, <u>home</u>, <u>pipe</u>, and <u>scene</u>.

1. Complete these sentences with list words that follow the unit pattern:

   a) I didn't real_ _ _ that I needed to dil_ _ _ the solvent first. If I had listened to your adv_ _ _ , I wouldn't have wasted the wh_ _ _ batch.

   b) There was great exc_ _ _ment at the Ch_ _ _se New Year celebration.

   c) You should ref_ _ _ to oper_ _ _ the car until the ch_ _ _ is repaired.

2. Moving from the outside circle to the centre, create words that contain a long vowel sound using the vowel-consonant-e pattern. Use each letter as often as possible. For example, s + a + f + e = safe.

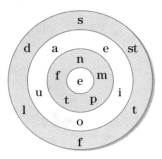

3. **a)** The prefix **uni-** means "one" or "single." Explain how this meaning applies to the following words: **universe**, uniform, united, unicorn, unique.

   b) The prefix **semi-** means "half" or "partially." Recall words with this prefix or use the dictionary to find examples. Does the meaning of each word fit the meaning of *semi*?

4. **Volume**, **sphere**, **whole**, and **bisect** are words used in mathematics. Do you know the meaning of these words? Look at the word webs below. Explain what you think each related word means. Check the dictionary if you are unsure.

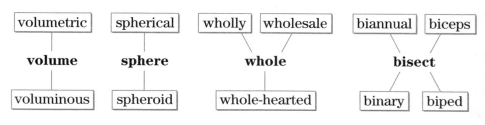

volumetric	spherical	wholly	wholesale	biannual	biceps
volume	**sphere**	**whole**		**bisect**	
voluminous	spheroid	whole-hearted		binary	biped

Writing and Revising

1. Prepare jot notes about the snowshoe hare or another animal.

   a) Research your animal using a variety of text and visual media.

   b) Record what you have learned in point-form notes.

   c) Include a picture or drawing of your animal with your notes.

2. Use your library resource centre to answer one or more of the following questions. Record your answers in point form.

   a) What **Chinese** leader started the first dynasty? For what is he famous (or infamous)?

   b) Even though Earth looks round, why isn't it a **sphere**?

   c) What is considered **polite** behaviour in your culture?

   d) How do scientists estimate the age of the **universe**?

3. **a)** Using your point-form notes, write a paragraph detailing your answer to one of the questions from the previous activity.

   b) Exchange your notes and paragraph with a partner. Which is easier to understand: your partner's paragraph or the notes? Explain why.

The Editing Desk

Pronouns Pronouns are words that take the place of, or stand for, nouns. By using pronouns, you avoid having to repeat the same noun over and over again. Your writing becomes more interesting and easier to read as a result.

In this excerpt from *Pit Pony* by Joyce Barkhouse, the pronouns are underlined:

❝ It was dark. He could hardly see the road. He looked up and saw a speck of light not far ahead. It was the first house he had seen for a long time. What would the folks say if he knocked at the door and said, "Please let me in." ❞

Here is a list of pronouns you probably use. They are called *personal pronouns* because they are words that stand for people or things.

Personal Pronouns

Self	I	me	my	mine
One Person or Thing	he / she	it / its	her / him	you / your
More Than One Person or Thing	we / us	they / them	you / your	their

1. **a)** Write a paragraph on any topic using some of the pronouns listed in the chart on page 7.

   b) What list word is a pronoun?

   Another type of pronoun is the *indefinite pronoun*. Indefinite pronouns are words that take the place of people and things that are not definitely named.

Indefinite Pronouns					
Less Than All	any	anybody	anyone	anything	few
All	all	every	everybody	everything	everyone

2. Choose a sample of your writing in which you have not used many or any pronouns. Rewrite the passage using personal and indefinite pronouns.

3. Many pronouns are used as the subject of a sentence, others follow prepositions. Choose the correct pronoun in parentheses for each of these sentences.

   a) (Us, We) waited under the shelter for the rain to stop.

   b) A man came up to (I, me) and handed (I, me) an envelope.

   c) What was this about? (I, me) wondered.

   d) "(We, Us) are having a promotion at Party Pizza," (he, him) said, looking at (us, we).

   e) For a moment, (he, him) stood there waiting.

   f) Were (we, us) supposed to give something to (he, him)?

   g) Then, it dawned on (we, us). (He, Him) was waiting for a tip!

L A N G U A G E   M A T T E R S

Can you complete these well-known movie and television lines with the correct pronoun?

- "Make _____ so, Number One." (Jean-Luc Picard, *Star Trek: The Next Generation*)
- "Beam _____ up, Scotty." (James T. Kirk, *Star Trek*)
- "_____ come in peace." (Buzz Lightyear, *Toy Story*)

3 Long Vowel Patterns

Many of the items on this shopping list are examples of words that follow a pattern other than vowel-consonant-e to create a long vowel sound. The only way to remember how to spell words like these is to memorize the various long-vowel-sound patterns (see Word Pattern).

Shopping List

macaroni
bay leaves
low-fat cheese
potato soup
cashews
wieners
diet cola

cucumbers
hand soap
fruit cocktail
blueberry pie
root beer
lightbulbs

Thinking about Words

agree
classify
complaint
conceited
continue
designer
disease
document
fuel
groan
photocopy
playoff
sigh
thrown
weighed

OTHER PATTERNS

*a lot
exactly
*friends
scissors
sizzle

1. These items from the shopping list contain the long **e** sound: low-fat cheese, wieners, bay leaves, macaroni, and root beer. Rewrite the underlined words in your notebook and circle the letters that create the long vowel sound /ē/ in each word.

2. The long **u** sound is sometimes pronounced /ü/ as in boot and /yü/ as in beautiful. Listen for these sounds in the following items from the shopping list:

cashews   fruit cocktail   potato soup
blueberry pie   root beer   cucumbers

Rewrite the words that contain the long vowel sound /ü/ and then circle the letters that create the sound in each word.

3. Find words in the shopping list that contain these vowel sounds:

a) long **o** (Five words. Hint: One word has two long **o** sounds.)

b) long **i** (Three words)

c) long **a** (Three words)

Word Pattern

Long vowel sounds can be created in a number of ways, such as the following:

/ā/ as in bait, **weighed**, play

/ē/ as in seen, beat, field, candy, kidney, receive, piano, sesame

/ī/ as in might, style, pilot, certify

/ō/ as in tomato, coating, bowling

/ü/or /yü/ as in blue, chewing, stupid, juicy, troops, few, **continue**

*frequently misspelled word

UNIT 3: LONG VOWEL PATTERNS **9**

1. a) Create a chart like the one below and write list words under the correct headings. (Hint: A word may appear under more than one heading.)

long /ā/	long /ē/	long /ī/	long /ō/	long /ü/
_____	_____	_____	_____	_____
_____	_____	_____	_____	_____
_____	_____	_____	_____	_____
_____				

b) Underline or highlight the letters that form the long vowel sound in each word.

2. The answers to the riddles below are pairs of rhyming words that contain a long vowel sound. Complete each rhyme with one of the list words. For example, insect's illness = bee's **disease**.

a) mild criticism = faint _____

b) calculated the mass of a green jewel = _____ jade

c) better decorator = finer _____

d) tossed dog toy = _____ bone

3. Say the word **sizzle** aloud. You can almost hear the sound of burgers cooking over an open flame! Many words seem to create vivid sounds and sight images as you say them. The technical term for this is *onomatopoeia*.

Substitute vivid words for the underlined verbs in the following sentences. Try to hear the sounds or see the images created by your onomatopoeic words. For example, "the waves hit the coastline" might become "the waves battered the coastline."

a) The water flowed from the tap.

b) My baby sister cried when we left the room.

c) The music from his radio wakened the neighbours.

d) The tree branches moved under the weight of the new snow.

4. Rewrite the list of words below. Say them aloud and notice which letters are silent or difficult to hear. To help you remember how to spell these words, circle or highlight any letters that need to be emphasized in pronunciation.

library	environment	escape
probably	pumpkin	**scissors**

SPELLING SECRETS

Some people remember the "c" in **scissors** by pronouncing the word *skissors*. This strategy may help you with other tricky words.

SPELLING SECRETS

A tip to help you remember that **a lot** is two words is to think of its opposite, *a little*.

1. Lists are series of words or phrases that are related in some way. A list often has no special order or meaning except to the person who made it. Here are some lists for you to make.

a) List everything you have seen from the moment you left your home to the time you arrived at school.

b) List every musical group you have ever liked.

c) List as many breeds of dogs (or cats) as you can.

d) List the types of appliances (both large and small) that people could have in their homes.

e) List all the car models you know.

2. Look at the shopping list on page 9. Add five more items that include a long-vowel-sound pattern. Exchange your list with a partner to ensure your spelling follows the correct pattern.

3. a) What do the following words have in common?

hazy	fog	sunny
rain	ice	bolt

b) Aside from the fact that all the words in part (a) are weather terms, they are also used in common expressions unrelated to the weather. Can you figure out which word completes these sentences?

• My memory is _____.

• He's in a _____.

• I'll have my eggs _____-side up, please.

• Can I have a _____ check?

• The meeting broke the _____.

• It was a _____ out of the blue.

The Editing Desk

Prepositions A preposition is a word that shows a relationship of time, position, or direction. It connects words in a sentence to other words. The chart at the top of page 12 lists some common prepositions.

Prepositions		
Time	**Position**	**Direction**
after	at	above
before	beside	across
since	between	down
until	for	over
	to	through
	with	under
	within	up

Notice the prepositions (underlined) in this passage from Jean Little's short story "The Training of Zephyr":

66 I have known a guide dog to snatch food <u>off</u> the table. I have met one who speedily became overprotective and is a worry when strangers come <u>around</u>. I have met one who barks loud and long when anyone goes <u>down</u> the hall <u>outside</u> the apartment <u>in which</u> he lives. 99

1. Prepositions help to make your writing more clear. Which preposition would you choose to complete the following sentences?

   a) Watch that you don't choke _____ that bone. (with, on)

   b) She awakened _____ the sounds of barking. (to, with)

   c) You can continue _____ the entire assignment. (with, on)

   d) We realized the paper was marked "Secret: _____ your eyes only!" (to, for)

2. Prepositions are often used incorrectly or left out altogether. Choose the correct sentence from each of the following pairs.

   a) There are a couple CDs I'd like to get.

   There are a couple of CDs I'd like to get.

   b) Jing-mei was suddenly frightened by the sound of the thunder.

   Jing-mei was suddenly frightened of the sound of the thunder.

   c) They shouted for me to hurry if I wanted to get inside the building.

   They shouted for me to hurry up if I wanted to get inside the building.

   d) Our class joined up with a class from another school.

   Our class joined a class from another school.

4 Syllables and Stress

When Kimiko glanced back at her diary entry she realized she had made a spelling error in the second sentence. Can you find it?

Notice the word <u>different</u>. Did you find the error? Kimiko probably left out one "e" because the middle syllable in *different* is often not pronounced.

date

Dear Diary

Grade 7 is great! There's so much more freedom, and we rotate to diffrent classrooms. I get to see my friends in the hallway even if they're not in my class.

I wish my locker was bigger, though. It's overflowing with notebooks, pencils, and notes from all my friends. My mirror fell off the door yesterday and smashed into a million pieces. I could've died!

Time to get ready for soccer.

Kimiko

1. concrete
2. content
3. contract
4. entrance
5. graduate
6. minute
7. moderate
8. proceeds
9. produce
10. project
11. record
12. refill
13. separate
14. subject
15. suspect

OTHER PATTERNS

16. *eighth
17. quarrel
18. Québec
19. question
*thoughts

Thinking about Words

1. Sort this list of words taken from the diary entry into three categories: two-syllable words, three-syllable words, and four-syllable words.

| yesterday | hallway | pieces |
| mirror | overflowing | freedom |

2. Do you say the word <u>rotate</u> with the stress on the first syllable or the second? Both pronunciations are correct.

The following words have been divided into syllables and appear as they would in a dictionary entry.

yes•ter•day   o•ver•flow•ing

Place a stress mark (´) over the syllable that receives the primary stress in each word. Consult a dictionary if you are unsure.

Word Pattern

discipline

In words containing more than one syllable, primary stress is usually placed on only one of the syllables.

1. All of the list words (excluding those under Other Patterns) can be pronounced two ways depending on which syllable is stressed. A different pronunciation can result not only in a change in vowel sounds, but in word meaning.

Write the list word that fits each pair of definitions that follow:

a) moves forward; money obtained from a sale

b) a point in time; very small or tiny

c) facts or ideas stated; satisfy or please

d) door or passageway; fill with joy

e) fruit and vegetables; bring into existence

2. Match list words with each of the following shapes:

3. Unscramble the syllables in the box below to find three two-syllable and three three-syllable list words.

ate	u	a	rate	mod
rel	sep	quar	er	con
grad	tract	tion	ques	ate

4. In English, the letter **q** is almost always followed by **u**, as in **question**, **quarrel**, and **Québec**. Unlike the place name Québec, however, not all place names containing a **q** follow it with a **u**.

Match each of these place names with their geographical location. Have an atlas handy!

Qandahar   Iran

Qatar   China

Qiqihar   state on the Persian Gulf

Qom   Afghanistan

1. Each list word (excluding those in Other Patterns) has two meanings and parts of speech depending on which syllable is stressed. For each of the following list words, write a sentence using both meanings.
For example, "With no more time left to research his topic, Ivan had to be **content** with the **content** of his report."

contract   project   record   suspect

2. Many diary entries start with *Dear Diary* (see p. 13). But what if the situation were reversed? What if your diary wrote to you? Write an entry you might get from your diary.

3. Write an imaginary diary entry for one of the following topics (or make up one of your own).

    a) on the road with a rock group

    b) the perfect summer holiday

    c) at the training camp of a professional sports team

    d) meeting friends after school

4. Rewrite the following diary entry. Substitute the underlined words and phrases with appropriate list words to make the entry more concise.

Dear Diary:

I have a suspicion that the fraction of an hour I step through the opening of my house, I'll get some good news. Maybe my sister—the one who finished her course of study from college—will be home for a visit. Or my dad will say he has just gotten a written agreement for a new job. At any rate, I'll be very satisfied with counting the money I received from our yard sale.

LANGUAGE MATTERS

Notice that the word **eighth** has four consonants together. Here are some other words with unusual combinations of vowels and consonants:

- Egypt (ē ′jipt): a country in Africa
- miaow (mē ou′): the sound a cat makes
- euchre (yü′kər): a card game for two to four players
- ouananiche (wä′nə nish′): a species of Atlantic salmon native to Lake St. John

---

The Editing Desk

Nouns Nouns are words that name people, places, and things. Here are two common classes of nouns:

Common nouns: names of places and things that are not capitalized, such as dog, books, river, apartment

Proper nouns: names of specific people and places that are capitalized, such as Marc Garneau, British Columbia, Mackenzie River, Riverview Drive, the CN Tower

Writers, of course, use lots of nouns. In this passage from *Whooping Crane Adventure* by Max Braithwaite, the common nouns are underlined once, the proper nouns twice.

ὦ It was four <u>days</u> after the dramatic <u>rescue</u> and <u>Jeff</u> still felt the <u>thrill</u> of the <u>plane</u> <u>ride</u>. The <u>pilot</u> had loaded the <u>hitchhiker</u> and his <u>accomplice</u>, the <u>kids</u> including <u>Tony</u>, and two <u>whoopers</u> [whooping cranes] into the <u>plane</u> and flown them back to the <u>Gardner</u> <u>camp</u>. ὧ

1. a) Write the list words that are nouns. Which list word is a proper noun?

   b) Choose a paragraph from one of your written assignments. Circle all the nouns. Have you used any proper nouns?

2. Do you know these expressions? Fill in the missing common nouns to complete each one. The meaning of the expression is in parentheses.

   a) walking on _____ (very happy or pleased)

   b) the writing is on the _____ (obvious; clear)

   c) just the tip of the _____ (more complicated than it seems)

   d) the calm before the _____ (something terrible is about to happen)

3. A *thesaurus* is a book of synonyms (words that mean the same or nearly the same thing). When you write, you may want to use a thesaurus to find nouns that are more colourful or descriptive.

   Rewrite the following passage, inserting more interesting nouns as you go along.

STROKE:
FLATTER...
MANIPULATE...
RUB...
TOUCH...

VIEY

THE THESAURUS REGATTA

9-18
©1996 Washington Post Writers Group   E-mail: SEQUITOON@aol.com
Reprinted with permission

It ended at eleven. We left the place and walked past the building. In a corner of the building, someone was standing under something. We couldn't see the person. Time to run down the street, we all decided!

5 Pronunciation Challenges

Can you spot the spelling errors in Danielle's letter? Why do you think these words were difficult to spell?

Notice the words <u>suprised</u>, <u>resterant</u>, <u>sanwich</u>, <u>pumkin</u>, and <u>rasberry</u>. Did you find the errors? When a letter in a word is not clearly pronounced, it is easy to make a mistake when spelling that word.

Dear Uncle Bryson,

I was suprised to find the gift certificate for my favourite resterant in my birthday card. It was a great idea! Colin and I went there yesterday for lunch. We each had a sanwich and dessert. I ordered pumkin pie and Colin had chocolate ice cream. I know if you had been there you'd have ordered rasberry pie!

Love,
Danielle

arctic
colonel
definite
depth
doughnuts
extinct
February
gnat
length
nuclear
recognize
rehearse
spaghetti
vacuum
Wednesday

OTHER PATTERNS
*caught
employee
moisture
noises
*turkey

Thinking about Words

1. **a)** Say the words <u>sandwich</u>, <u>pumpkin</u>, and <u>raspberry</u> just as you would normally say them. Say them again, but this time put special stress on those letters Danielle forgot to include.

   b) Correctly rewrite the five words that Danielle misspelled in her letter. Then circle, underline, or highlight in some way the letters Danielle missed.

2. The words <u>favourite</u> and <u>chocolate</u> were spelled correctly in Danielle's letter. Circle the letters in both words that are not pronounced clearly in everyday speech. Say these words aloud and stress the letters you circled.

Word Pattern

Spelling errors often occur with words that have unusual pronunciations or that are not pronounced clearly in everyday speech.

frequently misspelled word

1. Link the following shapes with list words:

2. Complete the following list words. Circle or highlight the letters you added. These letters are not always clearly pronounced in everyday speech. Say the words aloud, focussing on the highlighted letters.

    a) ar_tic   **b)** def_n_te   **c)** e_tin_t   **d)** Feb_uary

    e) nuc_ _ _r   **f)** reco_nize   **g)** reh_ _rse   **h)** vac_ _m

3. Sometimes it helps to mispronounce a word on purpose so that silent letters or hard-to-hear letters can be heard. How would you say these list words to help you recall the tricky letters?

    Wednesday   colonel   spaghetti   gnat   vacuum

4. The word **employee** means someone who is employed. An <u>employer</u> is the person who "employs" the employee. When **ee** is added to a base word, it often means "someone who is…."

    Try to define the following words. Use a dictionary if you are unsure.

    a) adoptee   **b)** interviewee   **c)** trainee   **d)** appointee

    e) nominee   **f)** refugee   **g)** parolee   **h)** trustee

---

LANGUAGE MATTERS

Words related to military rank are often not spelled the way they sound. Example: **colonel**, <u>sergeant</u>, <u>lieutenant</u>.

Writing and Revising

1. Letters are personal examples of writing. The form and tone of a letter, however, depends on who is going to read it. Write a letter of complaint to two of the following about a product you have purchased.

- the manufacturer
- the Letters to the Editor section of your local newspaper
- a friend who wants to buy the same product
- a humour magazine

2. The word **vacuum** is unusual not only because it is spelled with a double **u**, but because each **u** is often pronounced.

>   **a)** List three other words that contain a double vowel, each of which is pronounced separately. For example, <u>seed</u> or <u>balloon</u> don't fit this pattern because the double vowel has only one sound. (Hint: Think of words that have a hyphen separating the double vowels.)
>
>   **b)** Try writing a paragraph using the word *vacuum* along with the words you listed in the previous activity.

3. Black-flies are **gnats** that breed in fast-moving water in the forests of the Canadian Shield.

>   **a)** Find out more about the life cycle and habitat of black-flies. Write up what you have found in the form of a letter to someone in another country.
>
>   **b)** What other animal name starts with **gn**? (Hint: It's larger than a gnat and lives in Africa.)

Reprinted with permission—Toronto Star Syndicate
©1996 Tribuna Media Services

>   **4. a)** Rewrite the letter to Uncle Bryson (see p. 17) using at least five list words. (Change the subject of the letter if you like.)
>
>   **b)** Write a response that Uncle Bryson might send in reply.

The Editing Desk

Adjectives An adjective is a word that tells more about a noun or a pronoun. Here are some examples:

• In the phrase "broken windshield," <u>broken</u> describes the condition of the windshield.

• In the sentence "the music was too loud," <u>too</u> sets a limit on how loud the music was.

The adjectives (underlined) Susan Forest chose in this passage from her novel *The Dragon Prince* make the picture she is creating more vivid.

66 Beyond the <u>suffocating</u> whiteness, the mountains stretched out, jealously fencing her from the <u>familiar</u> lights she imagined in the distance. The forest would be <u>dark</u>, now. She shuddered. No, she would not follow the <u>wool</u> markers back through those <u>grey</u> woods tonight. **99**

1. Complete these sentences by adding interesting adjectives.

    a) It was a _____ and _____ night.

    b) The _____ wind made the _____ door creak and moan.

    c) Then I heard a _____ sound.

    d) Was it the _____ storm or some other _____ cry?

2. Adjectives, like any describing word, can be overused. Look at this piece of writing:

    The <u>greasy</u>, <u>torn</u>, and <u>ragged</u> bag of <u>hot</u>, <u>buttered</u> popcorn landed on the <u>blue</u> and <u>moldy</u> patch of <u>yellow</u>, <u>torn</u>, <u>wall-to-wall</u> carpet.

    By including so many adjectives, the main idea of the sentence is lost.

    a) Choose a piece of your own writing. Work with a partner to answer these questions:
    - What adjectives have you used?
    - Is the usage correct?
    - Does each adjective add to the meaning of the sentence?

    b) Revise the piece to make it more effective.

LANGUAGE MATTERS

Cryptic comes from the ancient Greek word *kryptos* meaning "hidden." So, a *crypt* is an underground or "hidden" burial vault. A *cryptogram* is a secret or "hidden" code of writing.

Here are some cryptograms to decipher:
- Bet her L8 the hen N.V. HER
- I B 4 E X Aft R C

- 10 decks SA cent hurry
- If U R not CMG, 2 bad 4 U

6 Review Units 1-5

1. Each of the following sets of words has some spelling feature in common. Complete each word, then state the common feature in the set. (Hint: Consider letter combinations, silent letters, and so on.)

   a) vac_ _m; employ_ _; proc_ _ds

   b) gra_ _; _ _otocopy; s_ _ere

   c) cla_ _ify; di_ _icult; refi_ _

   d) r_ythm; spag_etti; ex_ibit

2. a) Complete each of the following list words with either **gh**, **gu**, or **qu**.

dou_ _nuts	_ _arrel	_ _ébec	_ _estion	wei_ _ed
_ _ide	ei_ _th	throu_ _	_ _est	thou_ _ts

   b) Group the words from part (a) under the pattern headings **gh**, **gu**, and **qu**.

3. The following words are easily mispronounced. Examine the words carefully, then say each word aloud so that every sound is clearly pronounced in the correct order.

   nuclear   recognize   February

   arctic   depth   extinct

4. Schwa vowels, or vowels in unstressed syllables, are difficult to spell because they are not clearly pronounced. Rewrite the following words so that the underlined schwa vowel is highlighted in some way.

   helicopter   definite   separate

   difficult   fuel   universe

5. Which words in each set contain the long vowel sound shown?

   a) /ō/ thrown; thought; though; through

   b) /ē/ spread; scream; search; steering

   c) /ā/ weighed; height; eighth; neighbour

   d) /ī/ classify; cavity; exit; excite

Proofreading

How many misspelled list words can you find in this paragraph? Rewrite the paragraph and correct the errors.

The period between September and Febuary is allways my favourite time of the year. Why? It's basket ball season! First, there are the tryouts. Our coach works us really hard, but when we sigh that the drills are too dificult, she just growns and says, "No pain, no gain!" Evryone is soar after the first week, but as the season continue, it's not so bad. It all pays off in the playoffs. Last year we made it to the semifinals. I'll never forget the excitment I felt when I scored a basket in the final minit of the game. What I didn't relize was that I'd scored on my own net!

Dictionary Skills

Pronunciation Key Unit 5 contained some words with unusual pronunciations, but did you know a dictionary can help you pronounce such words?

Following each entry word in a dictionary is a phonetic version of how the word is pronounced. This information is usually in parentheses and relies on a code that represents each sound. The code is deciphered using a Pronunciation Key. Here is a sample key:

a	hat, cap	**h**	he, how	**ou**	house, out	**yü**	use, music
ā	age, face	**i**	it, pin	**p**	paper, cup	**v**	very, save
ä	barn, far	**ī**	ice, five	**r**	run, try	**w**	will, woman
				s	say, yes	**y**	young, yet
b	bad, rob	**j**	jam, enjoy				
ch	child, much	**k**	kind, seek			**z**	zero, breeze
d	did, red	**l**	land, coal	**sh**	she, rush	**zh**	measure,
		m	me, am	**t**	tell, it		seizure
e	let, best	**n**	no, in	**th**	thin, both		
ē	equal, be	**ng**	long, bring	**ŦH**	then, smooth	**ə**	represents:
er	care, bear						a in about
ėr	term, learn	**o**	hot, rock				e in taken
		ō	open, go	**u**	cup, butter		i in pencil
f	fat, if	**ô**	order, door	**u̇**	full, put		o in lemon
g	go, bag	**oi**	oil, voice	**ü**	rule, move		u in circus

The following are phonetic versions of words from Unit 5. Use the pronunciation key to identify the words.

(nat)　　(kėr´nəl)　　(nyü´klē ər)　　(rek´əg nīz´)

Language Power

Shades of Meaning　Words often carry meaning beyond their dictionary definitions. These added meanings, which are often charged with emotional power, are called the *connotations* of a word. For example, the word house is usually just thought of as meaning "a dwelling." The word home, however, carries many connotations. You may associate *home* with comfort, family, security. A nursing home, on the other hand, may have very negative connotations, depending on your experiences.

1. One word in each of the following pairs has positive connotations, the other negative. List all the positive words in one column, and all the negative words in another.

    thrifty / cheap　　　stubborn / determined　　　proud / conceited
    firm / bossy　　　　skinny / slim

2. Writers use the connotations of words as powerful tools. Write a short description of one of the following incidents. First, describe the event, making it seem as positive as possible. Then tell the story again using the same basic details, but this time, use words with negative connotations.

- You have just survived baby-sitting some children who were incredibly rude and destructive. Their parents return home and ask, "How did things go?"
- You are reporting on a sporting event for your school newspaper. The boys' soccer team lost the championship game to their rivals, the Central Cougars, 7-1.
- You are designing a real estate advertisement for the run-down house across the street.

Writing and Revising

1. Write the dialogue of a conversation that might take place between two characters. Use these list words in your dialogue:

| difficult | nonsense | always | advice | conceited |
| groan | eighth | suspect | definite | Wednesday |

2. a) Review the list words in Units 1–5. Think of ways to sort the words into categories. You might, for example, sort by

- length (four-letter words; five-letter words).
- part of speech (nouns; verbs; adjectives).
- subject or topic (useful objects; transportation; words that show emotion).
- difficulty (unusual spellings; words you know how to spell; words you need to learn).

b) Find at least five list words for each category.

3. Here are some words with different spellings for long vowels. Read the clues and then spell each word. Circle the letters that make the long vowel sound. (Hint: A dictionary can help you with these words.)

a)	the language of Portugal	P_rt_ _ _ _ _ _
b)	the ruler of ancient Egypt	p_a_ _ _ _
c)	a female sheep	e_e
d)	the hair right below your forehead	_y_ _r_w
e)	three singers make up this group	tr_ _
f)	some magazines publish twelve of these every year	_ss_ _s
g)	flowers can be arranged like this	b_ _q_ _ _

4. a) Research one of the topics below. (All the subjects are based on list words.) Write five interesting facts in point form about your research topic.

- prairie grasslands
- an auto-immune disease
- the age of the universe
- the first uses of concrete

b) Summarize what you have learned in the form of a letter. Imagine you are writing to someone who is working on a project about your topic.

c) Revise your letter so that it is just a paragraph of explanation, not a letter.

d) How are the two forms of writing different?

The Editing Desk

1. Find ten list words for each of the following parts of speech: noun, verb, adverb, adjective. Rewrite your list words in chart form under the correct headings.

2. Some words can act as a noun or an adjective, depending on how they are used. For example, the list word *sore* could refer to a symptom of pain or describe an area of broken skin. How many more list words can you find that fit the noun *and* adjective category?

3. How do you know which preposition should follow a word? Is it "angry at me" or "angry with me"? (It's "angry *with* me.")

Grammar rules for prepositions don't always make sense. How they are used often depends on current writing trends. Do you know which choice in parentheses best completes each sentence? (Not all of the words in parentheses are prepositions.)

    a) She is different _____ the rest of the kids in her class. (from, than)

    b) Finally, we all agreed _____ the change in plans. (with, to)

    c) The play was centred _____ the forwards crossing at the blue line. (around, on)

    d) The cat jumped _____ the table and ran across the room. (off, off of)

    e) We all shouted for him to _____, but he still didn't run. (hurry, hurry up)

    f) Our group's task was to investigate _____ of the experiment. (the results, into the results)

    g) _____ last year, our team hadn't lost a game. (Up until, Until)

4. The names of people are always capitalized unless they are functioning as common nouns. Do you know the common-noun meanings of these names?

    a) mike =   **b)** dolly =   **c)** beryl =   **d)** olive =

    e) victor =   **f)** jack =   **g)** bobby =   **h)** martin =

5. Choose a name from the previous activity and write a sentence using both the common and proper form of the noun. For example, "Bill suddenly realized he'd forgotten his wallet and couldn't pay the bill."

1. Here are some words that always seem to go together—like <u>milk</u> and <u>honey</u>. Can you fill in the missing word? Do you know what the expression means?

blue	carry	go	pains
bones	chips	order	take

a) give and _____   **b)** aches and _____

c) stop and _____   **d)** skin and _____

e) cash and _____   **f)** black and _____

g) fish and _____   **h)** law and _____

2. Try this word teaser. Write a word for each letter of the alphabet (or as many letters as you can) following these rules:

- Each word must begin and end with the same letter.
- You can use proper nouns and brand names.
- If you become stumped, use foreign words (*elle*) and acronyms (radar).

Here is an example: **area**
                                      Bob
                                        clinic
                                        dad
                                        elle
                                        f____f

3. How carefully do you read? Here are some brain teasers that depend on language. Can you do each one correctly?

a) A horse farm had nineteen stallions. All except eight died. How many were left?

b) If a car crashes on the border of Alberta, Saskatchewan, and the Western Arctic, where would the survivors be buried?

c) Would a rock sink more quickly in 10°C water or –5°C water?

d) Say these words out loud: BOAST, COAST, ROAST. What do you put in a toaster?

7 Schwa Vowels

Supreme Family Restaurant

Chef's Specialties*

Chicken fingers with fries ... **$8.95**

Lasagna **$9.65**

Fresh halibut steaks **$10.95**

Smoked salmon **$12.50**

* *Served with choice of broccoli or cauliflower*

Desserts

Lemon meringue pie ... **$3.25**

Muffin (assorted) **$0.85**

If you tried to spell all the words on this menu you might be biting off more than you could chew! Many of the words contain schwa vowels. These are vowels in unstressed syllables. Schwa vowels are often difficult to hear and cause many spelling errors.

account
among
award
cabinet
catalogue
ecology
federal
forgotten
individual
magazine
opinion
relatives
religious
sensible
skeleton

OTHER PATTERNS
*children
*machinery
wrecked
wrench
wriggle

Thinking about Words

1. Say the words <u>muffin</u>, <u>lemon</u>, <u>chicken</u>, and <u>salmon</u> aloud. Listen to the last syllable. The vowel sound you hear in each case is a schwa vowel.

   Rewrite these words and circle the schwa vowel. How many different ways is this type of vowel spelled?

2. The pronunciation symbol for schwa vowels is /ə/. Replace this symbol with the correct vowel letter in each of the words below:

   a) broccəli   **b)** ləsagna   **c)** cauləflower   **d)** haləbut

   Notice that even though the schwa vowel sounds almost identical in each word, the sound is spelled in three different ways.

Word Pattern

The vowel sound in many unstressed syllables is the schwa sound /ə/, as in the second syllable of <u>bacon</u> or <u>family</u>.

1. The blanks in the list words below each represent a schwa vowel. Rewrite the words and circle or highlight the letters you have supplied. Notice that the schwa sound can be spelled with any of the vowel letters. That's why it is so tricky!

  a) ecol_gy   **b)** sens_ble   **c)** relig_ _ _s

  d) m_chin_ry   **e)** ind_vidu_l

2. Unscramble the following syllables to make five three-syllable list words. The middle syllable in each word is a schwa vowel.

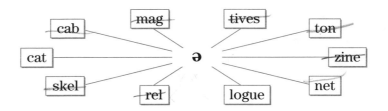

3. Complete the following analogies with list words:

  a) Province is to country as provincial is to _____.

  b) Remembered is to forgotten as silly is to _sensible_.

  c) Parents are to offspring as adults are to _____.

  d) Team is to athlete as group is to _____.

4. The list words **wrecked**, **wrench**, and **wriggle** all spell the sound /r/ with **wr**. Use the following clues to find other words from this family:

  a) a small bird: wr_ _

  b) homophone for what you wear on your finger: wr_ _ _

  c) opposite of right: wr_i_t_e

  d) connected to the hand: wr_i_s_t

  e) covering or cover: wr_ _ _ _ _

Writing and Revising

1. Behind every restaurant menu are good recipes. Using a food item of your choice, or one from the menu on page 27, find a recipe that contains your chosen item. Rewrite the recipe in your own words so that it is easy to understand.

Many expressions contain *food* words. How many of these food sayings do you know? Choose a word that fits the blank.

candy	nut	pudding
mustard	potato	sardines

the proof of the _____   a tough _____ to crack
can't cut the _____   a couch _____
packed like _____   like taking _____ from a baby

2. What kind of food would be served in the "wacky" restaurants listed below? Make up a sample menu for one of them.
   - The Whole Food Catalogue
   - The Federal Food Cabinet
   - Shipwrecked and Wriggled

3. **a)** A **catalogue** is a list of items in a collection. Think about items for which you have catalogues: books, music, stamps, coins, furniture, clothing, tools, and so on. Use the library to research types of catalogues or scan the ones you have at home.

   b) Create a catalogue for something you collect. Consider using word processing, spreadsheet, or database software to record your data. Here is one method you might use to catalogue your music collection.

Artist	CD / Cassette / Album	Label	Date of Recording	Comments

The Editing Desk

Sentences: Sentence Parts A sentence is a group of words that expresses a complete thought. Every sentence needs the following:

Subject: what the sentence is about

Action: what the subject is doing

Subjects are usually nouns or groups of words that act as nouns. Action words are verbs. For example, "I agree with you" is a sentence. *I* is the subject and *agree* is the action or verb. The words *with you* complete the sentence by telling something about *I agree*.

Sentences can be made up of one word or many words. How many sentences are there in this paragraph from Martyn Godfrey's *Mystery in the Frozen Lands*?

66 That means that the ships were abandoned. But why? Why were they dragging a boat across the ice to the south? Why did they vanish? Why?

Only the thought that I will know the answers very soon finally allows me to sleep. **99**

1. Choose six list words and write a sentence for each word. Label the subject and action words in your sentences. (Hint: Some action words can be made up of two words.)

2. Complete these sentences with either a subject or an action word where indicated.

   a) Cleaning up a _attic_ (subject) can be easy if you know how.

   b) First _get_ (action) a bunch of garbage bags and boxes.

   c) Put anything you _want_ (action) into bags. These you will _throw_ (action) away.

   d) Once the _attic_ (subject) is empty, _repaint_ (action) the door.

   e) Don't let anyone in, not even _children_ (subject)!

   f) That way your _attic_ (subject) will stay _neat_ (action) forever.

8 Homophones

Do you think the two spelling errors in this ad are really mistakes? If not, why did the writer purposely use the wrong homophone spelling for <u>sale</u> and <u>not</u>?

28.8 (V.34) cellular fax/modem.

BOAT FOR SAIL!

7 m Olympic Keele boat, 3 sails, compass, life jackets, etc. $3000.00.

KNOT TO BE MISSED!

14" Colour Tv, stereo sound with

allowed
aloud
flour
hangar
hanger
pore
pour
stationary
stationery
steal
steel
waist
ware
waste

OTHER PATTERNS
*instead
loose
lose
receipt
recipe
*Saturday

Thinking about Words

1. Advertisers often play with the spelling of words to create interest. The following businesses specialize in hairstyling. The owners have used homophones or unusual spellings to create a humorous effect.

Write the names of these businesses as they should be spelled:

a) Shear Delights

b) Curl Up and Dye

c) Hairloom Hairstyling

d) Rico's Hairitage

2. Try creating your own humorous advertisement using some of the homophone list words.

Word Pattern

Words that sound the same but have different meanings, and sometimes different spellings, are called *homophones*.

1. Complete the following sentences with the correct homophone pairs. (Hint: At least one of the homophones in each sentence appears in the unit list.)

a) We are not _____ to sing _____ while the baby is sleeping.

b) Is that beautiful _____ made out of _____ and water?

c) I left my jacket on a _____ when our class toured the _____ at the airport.

d) The special belt for my _____ was really a _____ of money.

2. Match the correct pair of homophones with each of the clues.

1. plain/plane	**a)** a faded bucket
2. pale/pail	**b)** writing paper that doesn't move
3. herd/heard	**c)** the cattle paid attention
4. steal/steel	**d)** ordinary-looking airline
5. heals/heels	**e)** the work done by a foot doctor
6. stationary/stationery	**f)** take the alloy of iron and carbon without permission

3. Use the words **receipt** and **recipe** in one or more sentences to show that you understand the meaning of each.

4. There are many English idioms or expressions that contain the word **lose**. Write in your own words what you think each of the following sentences means.

a) You'll lose your shirt if you invest in that company.

b) You stand to lose a great deal of money if you quit your job.

c) Don't lose heart. I'm sure we can solve this problem.

d) Don't lose your head when someone tries to start a fight.

LANGUAGE MATTERS

Many words are easily confused because of slight differences in spelling. For example:

human/humane	capital/capitol	set/sit
emigrant/immigrant	adapt/adopt	persecute/prosecute

Writing and Revising

1. The person who wrote this want ad must have been confused! Rewrite it using the correct words.

> **COT AGE FOUR SAIL** Why weight! Let yore imagination sore.
> Stay a weak, stay a lifethyme. Too bedrooms. To bathes.
> Basque under sum fur trees while you smell the sent of nature.
> By before those chili nights are hear. Call know! 222-1234.

2. Want ads are usually brief and use abbreviations or short forms of words. Find a want ad that looks interesting. Rewrite it using complete sentences. Give your ad a title.

3. Businesses often use unusual spelling, homophones, or incorrect words to advertise their products or services. Sometimes these words are part of a trademark or business title; for example, Kwik Kleen Laundry.

Reprinted with permission. All rights reserved.

  a) Collect a scrapbook of unusual business and product names.

  b) Why do you think businesses use these examples of incorrect spelling?

4. a) Re-arrange the letters of the words below to find common homophones.

nets	lates	leer
hewer	lima	rose

b) Write a sentence for each homophone.

c) Now add the matching homophone to each of your sentences. Example: Sitting on a <u>board</u> can make you very <u>bored</u>!

Recall the spelling of the word **loose** by thinking of a *loose moose*.

Here are some homophone words that are unusual. By re-arranging the letters in each word *or* by dropping a letter, you can create the matching homophone.

great	knight	hour	steak
bear	tide	fined	waive

The Editing Desk

Sentence Parts: Phrases A phrase is a group of words that does not express a complete thought. For example, "Going past the corner" is a phrase because the subject is missing. We don't know *who* is going past the corner.

1. Rewrite the paragraph below by changing the phrases into complete sentences. (Hint: You will have to add words to make a phrase a complete sentence.)

> The top of the hill seemed hours away. Nadia, her head down as she pedalled. The other bikers behind her. She looked back. Moving on the outside of the road. Breathing heavily. Her muscles in her legs. Coming to the end of the race.

2. a) Why do you think phrases are more difficult to understand than sentences?

   b) Create a list of words and phrases and then exchange your list with a partner. Challenge him or her to turn your words and phrases into complete sentences.

   c) Circle all the subject words and underline all the action words in your partner's sentences.

3. Explain what you think each one of these common expressions means. Rewrite those expressions that are phrases in the form of a complete sentence.

a) off the record	**b)** you said a mouthful
c) don't eat like a horse	**d)** a greasy spoon
e) get off my back	**f)** measure up to his older sister

9 Base Words

These are some basic facts about solar energy. With further research, you could build on these facts.

Similar to the way facts can build up with additional research, words can be built from basic parts called *base words*. Base words can be made larger by adding prefixes and suffixes.

Can you find any long words in the fact card that are based on smaller base words?

Solar Energy

- The energy that comes directly from the sun is a tremendous resource.

- Scientists are studying ways to convert solar power into enough electricity to supply a city's needs.

- In space, satellites and space stations get their energy from solar cells called "photovoltaics."

accept
oppose
appear
assist
calculate
compose
courage
depend
forgive
nature
refer
rely
reside
response
scope

OTHER PATTERNS

allowance
blouse
*choir
discount
*medicine

Thinking about Words

1. List as many words as you can think of that have <u>energy</u>, <u>sun</u>, or <u>convert</u> as their base word. Example:

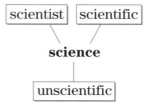

2. a) The words <u>directly</u> and <u>electricity</u> are built on smaller base words. What is the base word for each?

b) Record other words that are formed from the base words listed in part (a). For example, the word <u>direction</u> uses the same base as <u>directly</u>.

Word Pattern

Base words are words to which prefixes, suffixes, or other endings can be added. Prefixes are added to the beginning of a base word, suffixes to the end.

Working with Words

1. The /əns/ sound at the end of a base word can be spelled **-ance** or **-ence**. The following words all contain the /əns/ ending. Use a dictionary to help you figure out which ending fits each word.

a) accept_nce   **b)** appear_nce   **c)** assist_nce

d) depend_nce   **e)** refer_nce   **f)** resid_nce

2. Some base words can take a variety of prefixes. The answers to the riddles below all share the base word **scope**. Double check the spelling with a dictionary.

a) Some people think I can predict your future based on your time of birth.   _ _ _ _scope

b) I am a viewing device used in submarines.   _ _ _ _scope

c) I am used to magnify objects that are not visible to the naked eye.   _ _ _ _ _scope

d) Your doctor uses me to listen to your heartbeat.   _ _ _ _ _ _scope

3. Create as many new words as you can by linking the following base words and suffixes together. Remember, some suffixes can be combined with more than one base word. (Hint: The spelling of the base word may have to change when the suffix is added.)

Base Words		Suffixes	
forgive	calculate	-ment	-ness
nature	depend	-tion	-al
compose	response	-ition	-ible
courage	rely	-er	-able
oppose		-ous	

4. Say the words <u>medic</u> and medicine. Notice how the /k/ sound in medic becomes an /s/ sound in medicine. Even though the sound changes, the spelling remains the same. Remembering the base word will help you to spell medicine.

Say each of the following words aloud. Then write the words and circle the base words.

plasticize   magician   politician   electrician   optician

SPELLING SECRETS

Think of the base word each time you are adding a prefix or suffix. This is an important strategy in becoming a mature speller.

1. The idea of transforming solar energy into electricity was once considered science fiction. Now, solar energy is used in a number of ways and devices (see p. 35). Research a practical use for solar energy. Create a fact card on which you briefly describe what you have learned. Be sure to use complete sentences in your description and include a bibliography of your resources.

2. a) List as many words as you can based on the word <u>person</u>. There are at least ten.

b) Use all your *person* words in one paragraph.

3. Use a computer publishing program, if possible, to create a fact card for a topic that interests you. Use the example on page 35 as a model, or design one of your own. Consider attaching a photo or illustration related to your topic to the back of your fact card.

The Editing Desk

Punctuation Punctuation signals the reader to a break in a phrase or sentence. It also indicates the type of sentence. Here are some examples of common punctuation:

Period (.): ends a sentence

Comma (,): can be used to separate phrases, words in a list, and sentences connected by a conjunction. The comma is also used with quotation marks.

Question mark (?): comes at the end of a phrase or sentence that is worded in the form of a question

Exclamation mark (!): used at the end of a phrase or sentence that expresses a strong emotion

Colon (:): often used before a list of words or phrases

Which of the marks listed above are not used in this passage from Nazneen Sadiq's novel *Heartbreak High*?

  66 He had a beautiful shirt on. Tariq's tanned face and dark hair looked so vibrant against the deep blue! Rachel decided that his good looks must dazzle everyone around him. Did he know it? 99

1. When it is used correctly, punctuation makes writing more readable. Rewrite the following passage and insert the correct punctuation.

June 27

Today is moving day and everything is in a mess Why couldn't we have been better organized What a pile of confusion Just imagine books dishes toys knick-knacks garden tools shoes boots lamps and clothes Can you believe all this stuff The only thing I can say is that unpacking is easier I hope we can find everything The last time we moved I lost my two favourite CDs and I didn't find them until today Now is that crazy or what

B.C.   **by johnny hart**

By permission of Johnny Hart and Creators Syndicate, Inc.

2. As the above cartoon illustrates, an unnecessary or misplaced comma can have disastrous or humorous results. Compare the following sets of sentences. Which one do you think is correct in each pair?

a) Remember two wrongs, don't make a right.

Remember, two wrongs don't make a right.

b) When you are sending mail, friends, don't forget the postal code.

When you are sending mail, friends don't forget the postal code.

c) You must not remain, uninformed citizens.

You must not remain uninformed, citizens.

d) To Marc, Anthony's guitar work was the best he had ever heard.

To Marc Anthony's guitar work was the best he had ever heard.

10 Compound Words

When Isabel read this notice posted in the cafeteria, she thought some of the words were misspelled, but she wasn't sure. Can you find the three spelling errors in the notice?

Look carefully at these words as they are spelled on the poster: extrodinary, pinapple, earings. All of these words are compound words. When you realize a word is a compound word, spelling it is much easier.

For example: extra + ordinary = extraordinary

pine + apple = pineapple

ear + rings = earrings

Charity Auction

Come to the sixth annual Charity Auction, to be held on November 9 at Laurier Junior High School. Proceeds go to the Grant a Wish fund.

Items include

🛼 a pair of skates once worn by Canada's extrodinary men's figure skater Elvis Stojko.

⚾ a baseball signed by Joe Carter and his teammates.

📞 a telephone shaped like a pinapple.

💍 custom-designed earings.

See you there!

cell phone
earring
extraordinary
graveyard
hatchback
headache
nighttime
overdue
pineapple
spokesperson
teammate
touch-tone
uproar
wastebasket
windshield

OTHER PATTERNS
*kneel
*parallel
radar
R.S.V.P.
scuba

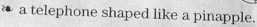

Thinking about Words

1. This notice isn't totally hopeless! What two compound words are spelled correctly?

2. Pronounce these words: shortstop / short stop
   What did you notice about the way you said them? The stress for *shortstop* is on the first syllable (shôrt´stop´). For *short stop*, the stress is almost equal. What pronunciation rule helps you decide when words are compound words?

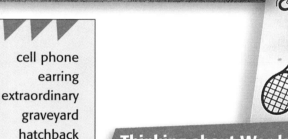

Word Pattern

Compound words are made up of two or more separate words that are usually related in meaning. Sidewalk, football, and **teammate** are all compound words.

1. Because compound words are really two words joined together in some way, they can have odd spelling patterns, like **nighttime**. Look at these words:

bookkeeper	**extraordinary**	hitchhike	**pineapple**
earring	glow-worm	jack-knife	throughout

a) Circle the letters where the two separate words are joined.

b) What letter combinations look unusual?

2. Compound words can be made up of any part of speech: noun, adjective, adverb, verb. The following list of small words has been organized under one possible part of speech. Use these small words to create as many compound words as you can.

Nouns	Adjectives	Adverbs	Verbs
speaker	some	where	melt
wind	loud	down	flash
shield	glow	up	diving
worm	no		light
hand	cell*		roar
sky			phone

* the word *cell* in this case is short for *cellullar*

3. Not all words containing smaller words are compound words. The word <u>carpet</u> is just one example. Which of the following words are not compound words? Explain why.

bandit	carnation	**headache**	season	tablet
bargain	downsize	carton	suitcase	**wastebasket**

4. Rewrite the four list words that have double consonants.

HUMMINGBIRD

A SONGBIRD THAT FORGOT THE WORDS

WILEY'S DICTIONARY

©1993 CREATORS SYNDICATE, INC.

By permission of Johnny Hart and Creators Syndicate, Inc.

1. The announcement below was taped to a telephone pole at a busy intersection. If the sale is fifty percent off, so is the writing. There are twelve spelling errors involving compound words. Can you find them all?

SIDE WALK SALE

Nightime is the rightime for this sale. Every one is wellcome to our annual sales event. Every thing is halfprice through out the store. But don't worry, we'll still make a profit. (Just ask our bookeeper!)
• Free dough nuts and marsh mallows for the kids
• Bring a suit case to cart away your savings

Sale ends this Saturday.

2. The list word **uproar** means "a noisy disturbance." Write about a time when you caused an uproar in your family. Try to include compound words in your story.

3. Make a scrapbook of flyers that come to your house and include any other notices that you find interesting. Try writing a notice of your own to promote, for example,

- a garage or yard sale.
- an employment opportunity (classified ad).
- a meeting or event.
- a specific product.
- the search for a lost pet.

Conjunctions Conjunctions are words that connect words, sentences, and phrases. Some common conjunctions include *and, but, for, nor, or, so, yet.*

- In the sentence, "The parade and the concert were cancelled" the conjunction <u>and</u> connects two nouns (*parade* and *concert*) with an action (*were cancelled*). Both were cancelled.

- In the sentence, "I was late for the bus, so I missed the movie" the conjunction <u>so</u> connects two sentences together (*I was late for the bus* and *I missed the movie*). In this example, the first sentence explains the second.

1. Unscramble the letters in the following nonsense sentence to find common prepositions and conjunctions. Each letter can only be used once to create a total of seven words.

O bail fast Cath! Dean is untrue.

2. Like the conjunction <u>and</u>, each of these other joining words can be used to join two supporting phrases or sentences together. Write a sentence for each one.

a) also	**b)** as well as	**c)** in fact
d) similarly	**e)** indeed	**f)** furthermore

3. The conjunction <u>but</u> is used to connect two opposite phrases or sentences together: "We arrived after eight o'clock, *but* by then it was too late."

Here are six joining words that can connect two opposing words, sentences, or phrases. Use each one in a sentence.

a) yet	**b)** while	**c)** despite
d) nevertheless	**e)** although	**f)** however

LANGUAGE MATTERS

Many new words that enter the language are related to technology. Some of these "technology" words are old words that have been given new meanings.

- Just leave it on the <u>machine</u>.
- We've been trying to <u>page</u> you all evening.
- My screen is <u>frozen</u>.
- I don't have enough <u>RAM</u> to open it.

Congradulations Rams! District Volleyball Champs!

Did you catch the spelling mistake on the banner? Why do you think the word **congratulations** was misspelled?

anxious
buoy
canoe
circuit
congratulations
conquer
feud
forty
leisure
mortgage
penguin
rescue
skiing
surgeon
tongue

OTHER PATTERNS
disappeared
*field
impatient
*probably
unpopular

Thinking about Words

1. Many people are challenged by the spelling of the word **congratulations** because it is a long word and the first /t/ sound is not always clearly pronounced. Developing tricks for recalling unusual spellings is often helpful. You could, for example, shorten *congratulations* to *congrats* where the /t/ sound is more obvious.

Can you add any other strategies for remembering the "t" in *congratulations*?

2. Create a brief announcement that might have been broadcast over the school's P.A. system praising the Rams on their big win. Try to use some of the list words in your announcement, such as **anxious**, **conquer**, **feud**, **forty**, and of course, **congratulations**.

Word Pattern

It is important to use a variety of spelling strategies for words that have unusual spellings.

Working with Words

1. Many of the list words contain unusual vowel combinations. Complete each word below. Then circle or highlight the letters you added.

a) surg_ _n   **b)** tong_ _   **c)** b_ _y

d) circ_ _t   **e)** conq_ _r   **f)** peng_ _n

g) resc_ _   **h)** f_ _d   **i)** can_ _

2. Unscramble the syllables in the box to spell five list words.

bly	la	ap	a	tions
u	im	grat	tient	dis
u	pop	pear	ed	prob
pa	con	lar	un	

3. The word **tongue** is used in several common expressions or idioms. Try to explain in your own words what the following idioms mean.

a) I knew why Anook was not at school, but I decided to hold my tongue.

b) Her name is on the tip of my tongue.

c) I'm sorry I called you Helena instead of Alana. It was just a slip of the tongue.

d) As soon as I mentioned Raoul's party to her, I could have bitten my tongue.

4. Write as many synonyms as you can for the list words **anxious**, **conquer**, **feud**, and **leisure**.

Consult a thesaurus and add any other synonyms that aren't already on your list.

5. Write the list words that match these shapes. Pay special attention to the consonants above and below the line.

6. Which list word has a homophone? Write both the list word and its homophone.

SPELLING SECRETS
. . . .
Notice that **leisure** is an exception to the rule *i* before *e* except after *c*.

1. Double consonants are among several unusual spelling patterns that challenge many writers. Use the clues below to help you unscramble these double-consonant words. Then, write a "memory trick" for each one to help you remember the spelling.

a) sradsed (You might write this on the outside of an envelope.)

b) nospisoses (Something you own or have)

c) resarabdems (Your face is red when you feel like this.)

d) rialglo (An endangered African primate)

2. Signs are short forms of communication. Sometimes they only consist of one or two words. What do the road signs below mean? Write your explanation in sentence form.

a) Be prepared to stop   **b)** Right lane must exit

c) Soft shoulders   **d)** Caution: Falling rocks

3. Make a scrapbook of interesting signs you have seen that contain a "blooper" or a clever use of words like this sign. If possible, include photographs of the signs.

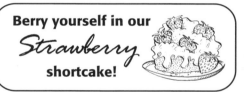

Berry yourself in our *Strawberry* **shortcake!**

4. What's wrong with these signs? Write your answer in sentence form.

a) Don't take this sale for granite

b) All dogs must be on leash no longer than 2.5 km

c) Buypass nest exit

d) Breakfeast served all day

e) No parking. Car's towed at owner's expense and will be prosecuted

The Editing Desk

Adverbs You can use adverbs to describe or modify a verb, another adverb, or an adjective. Many adverbs end in **-ly**. Example:

• She raced <u>quickly</u> up the stairs. *Quickly* modifies the verb *raced*.

• The wind blew <u>so</u> fiercely. *So* modifies the adverb *fiercely*, which tells something about the verb *blew*.

• David is an <u>extremely</u> helpful person. *Extremely* modifies the adjective *helpful*, which tells something about the noun *person*.

The adverbs have been underlined in this excerpt from Grace Richardson's novel *Into That Darkness Peering*:

66 The handle was <u>so</u> <u>deeply</u> rusted now, there seemed to be nothing to it but rust. Marnie grabbed it with her mittened hand and gave it several fierce tugs. <u>Abruptly</u>, the door burst open. 99

1. Rewrite the following sentences, replacing the blanks with some of these adverbs (or adverbs of your own): beautifully, suddenly, remarkably, quickly, sickly, unusually, extremely. (Hint: More than one adverb might work in any given blank.)

a) Slumber Beauty Cologne makes you smell like a(n) _____ fake flower. (modifies the adjective *fake*)

b) Splash it _____ on your face. (modifies the verb *splash*)

c) Don't be _____ alarmed if your eyes grow heavy. (modifies the verb *alarmed*)

d) It's a(n) _____ long rest worth taking! (modifies the adjective *long*)

2. Not all adverbs end in **-ly**. Use the adverbs listed in the box to complete the paragraph that follows.

almost	more	before
never	straight	still

The traffic stopped _____ we had time to swerve out of the way. I have _____ seen anything like it. Cars bounced off one another like billiard balls. We headed _____ for the ditch but _____ hit the truck in front of us. It was _____ impossible to believe no one was hurt. There were _____ smashed bumpers and fenders than in a car-chase movie.

LANGUAGE MATTERS

The words <u>well</u> and <u>good</u> are two describing words that can really drive you crazy! *Well* is an adverb, *good* is an adjective.

To figure out which one of these words to use, first identify what is happening in the sentence. What kind of word is being modified?

• For an action or other word that isn't a noun, use *well*. For example, "She plays basketball well."

• For a noun or subject word, use *good*. For example, "This is a good movie."

Working with Words

1. The following words contain schwa vowels in the unstressed syllables. Complete each word, then highlight the vowels you have added.

   a) med_cine   **b)** par_llel   **c)** sens_ble

   d) rel_tives   **e)** cat_logue   **f)** mag_zine

   g) skel_t_n   **h)** cab_net   **i)** prob_bly

2. Choose the correct homophone from the pair in parentheses to complete each of the following sentences:

   a) We used _____ to make the dough, then shaped it into a _____. (flower/flour)

   b) This is a test, so you are not _____ to shout the answers _____. (allowed/aloud)

   c) I don't want to _____ this fudge, but I'm trying to watch my _____line. (waist/waste)

   d) This old kitchen_____ is certainly showing signs of _____. (ware/wear)

3. The sounds /ər/ and /èr/ can be spelled in a number of ways, as shown by these list words. Complete each word with the correct spelling of the /ər/ or /èr/ sound.

/ər/	/èr/
Sat_ _day	s_ _geon
machin_ _y	spokesp_ _son
fed_ _al	c_ _cuit
conqu_ _	ref_ _

SPELLING SECRETS

· · · · · · ·

o you have trouble with e "u" in **Saturday**? Just ay to yourself, *U love aturday!*

4. Create a word web for one of the following words by adding prefixes, suffixes, or other word parts to the base word: appear, accept, compose, forgive.

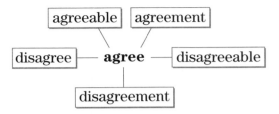

Proofreading

Rewrite the following passage, correcting any errors in spelling:

> Last Saterday night I was baking cookies. I was in a hurry and added two cups of flower insted of one. To make the batter smoother, I pored in some milk. The recipee didn't mention milk, but I figured some creativity would probally be aloud. While waiting for the cookies to bake, I read my favourite magizine. Twenty minutes later, I heard the smoke detector screech and knew I had forgoten the cookies. They were totally recked! It was a waist of my time and the ingredients. Next time, I'll try not to be so impaitent.

Dictionary Skills

Syllables Longer words are often easier to spell if we break them into syllables. There are complex and often confusing rules for dividing words into syllables. A dictionary does the dividing for you. Entry words are printed with a midline dot between each syllable. Example: dis•ap•pear

1. Divide these list words into syllables. Use a dictionary to help you.

    a) catalogue   **b)** stationary   **c)** probably   **d)** unpopular

Stress Patterns A dictionary provides information on which syllables are stressed when pronouncing the word. In shorter words, one syllable may be stressed. This syllable is marked with a primary stress symbol (ˊ) usually positioned after the syllable. Example: chil•dren (chilˊdrən).

    Longer words often have one syllable that has primary stress and one that has secondary stress. A bold accent (ˊ) indicates the syllable with primary stress, and a lighter accent (ˊ) marks the syllable that has secondary stress.

2. **a)** Consult your dictionary, then place the correct stress marks beside the syllables in the words from the previous activity.

b) Notice how many of the syllables in your answers contain schwa /ə/ vowels. As you learned in Unit 7, schwa vowels are found in most unstressed syllables. Because the vowels are not clearly pronounced, spelling words that contain the schwa sound is more difficult.

Circle the schwa vowels in the syllables from part (a).

Language Power

Clichés A cliché is a worn-out expression. When a saying is used over and over in speech or in writing, it becomes "tired" and seems to lack freshness.

1. The following expressions are considered clichés. How many of them can you complete? Ask a friend if you have difficulty.

a) take it or _____   **b)** a bottomless _____

c) too good to be _____   **d)** so far, so _____

e) a chip off _____   **f)** here today, _____

2. Similes are comparisons using *like* or *as*. We often use the same similes over and over again to express emotions or states rather than thinking of fresh comparisons. These over-used similes then become clichés.

What clichés are represented by these comparisons? (Hint: They all refer to animals.) In each case, complete the cliché, then create a new simile that would be more effective.

a) gentle as a _____   **b)** stubborn as an _____

c) free as a _____   **d)** hungry as a _____

e) sick as a _____   **f)** snug as a _____

Writing and Revising

1. Rewrite the following paragraph and replace each underlined word with the correct homophone.

Last <u>weak</u>, I started a pottery <u>coarse</u>. At first it <u>seamed</u> <u>two</u> much <u>too</u> learn. You had to shape the clay into a <u>bole</u>, making sure to <u>need</u> it carefully. Then you had to <u>throe</u> it on the <u>weal</u> and fire it in the kiln. But after a few <u>daze</u>, I <u>cot</u> on to it. The <u>wheal</u> is just <u>peddle</u> driven, and at first that was a difficult <u>lessen</u> to learn.

2. **a)** Write the meaning of each of these list words: ecology, steel, medicine, cell phone, canoe.

    b) Choose one of the words and write two interesting facts about it.

3. Some of the words below are compound words, others are not. Can you figure out which ones are which?

    a) all + right = compound word or not?

    b) for + ever = compound word or not?

    c) any + one = compound word or not?

    d) a + lot = compound word or not?

    e) every + time = compound word or not?

    f) every + body = compound word or not?

4. Words with silent letters can be difficult to spell. Can you find at least five list words from Units 7 through 11 that have a silent letter other than a silent e at the end of the word? (Hint: There are at least ten.)

5. Words and slogans that appear in visual displays (posters, ads, menus, and so on) are used to communicate a clear message to the reader. Find a display that appeals to you and answer the following questions:

    a) Why do you find the display interesting?

    b) What words and/or phrases explain its message?

The Editing Desk

1. Match a subject word (noun) with an action word (verb). Then write a sentence for each word pair. (Hint: Some subject words can also be adjectives and verbs. Make sure you use them correctly. You may also need to add a suffix to the action word.)

Subject (noun)	Action (verb)
award	wrecked
magazine	lose
receipt	pour
waste	forgive
courage	rely
nature	oppose
hatchback	disappeared
spokesperson	wriggle
penguin	calculate

2. Rewrite the following paragraph, inserting the proper punctuation. (Hint: Here are the types of punctuation marks that are missing: . , ? ! :)

> Wow I just couldn't believe what happened We were walking down the street and we stopped for a traffic light All of a sudden this great white limo pulls up blocks the intersection and stops traffic I'd never seen such a long limo Who could be inside We waited but no one got out and the limo didn't move Christine thought it was just a high-school grad party Naz didn't agree He said there were three possibilities a rock star a foreign official a sports celebrity Well would you believe he was wrong on all three guesses Suddenly Kim jumped out of the car Kim Then I remembered that her dad owned a limousine service

3. Substitute one of the following adverbs for the blanks in the paragraph below, or use an adverb of your own. (Hint: Some of these adverbs will work in more than one sentence.)

leisurely	quietly	definitely	suddenly
accidentally	quickly	painfully	merrily

> It was like slow motion. The ball rolled _____ toward the net. Only seconds before, the goalie had _____ slipped. Now she lay _____ as if she were watching the ball in a dream. Everyone _____ turned in the direction of the net, but it was _____ too late! I _____ twisted my leg when I tried to move toward the ball. I saw two other teammates _____ crash into each other. All the while, the ball kept rolling _____ along.

4. Use a conjunction and a comma to join each pair of sentences below.

   a) The ball landed on the green three hundred metres away. It rolled toward the hole.

   b) The crowd started to cheer. The ball didn't go into the cup.

   c) It spun around the rim three times. Like a jet plane, it shot off in another direction.

   d) Everyone watched in amazement. The ball kept rolling and rolling.

   e) It ended up twenty metres from the hole. The match was still won.

1. Palindromes are words or phrases that are spelled the same both forward and backward. People have been trying to create them since the early 1600s. Here are some examples:

did   tot   pop   mom

a) Write five words that are palindromes.

b) Try to write a short phrase or sentence that reads the same forward and backward. Here are some examples:

- O no!
- Madam, I'm Adam.
- And maybe the most famous of all: "A man, a plan, a canal, Panama!" about the building of the Panama Canal one hundred years ago.

2. Perfect word squares have the same words going down as across. People as far back as those in ancient Greece and Rome enjoyed making them. Here is a two-letter example. Can you make up one with three-letter words?

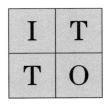

3. How many of these ten abbreviations do you know?

a) e.g.	**b)** IQ	**c)** R.S.V.P.	**d)** DJ	**e)** C.O.D.
f) MPP	**g)** H.R.H.	**h)** AC	**i)** TNT	**j)** p.m.

4. Here are two-word expressions where the second word rhymes with the first. Can you complete each one and explain what it means? (Clues are given for the first two.)

a) true _____ (a colour)

b) big _____ (false hair)

c) phony _____

d) fender _____

e) pay _____

f) fat _____

Plurals -s endings

by Brian Basset

Did you catch the spelling error in this cartoon? The misspelled word is spelled correctly in the word list.
Why do you think the plural of <u>potato</u> is often misspelled?

adults
audiences
capsules
citizens
desserts
echoes
heroes
matches
mosquitoes
mountains
potatoes
refugees
scratches
tomatoes
vegetables

OTHER PATTERNS
*all right
*captain
data
halves
women

Thinking about Words

1. We normally make words plural by adding **-s** to the singular form. For example, <u>mask</u> becomes <u>mask**s**</u>, orange becomes <u>orange**s**</u>, and so on. This pattern also works with some words ending in **o**.

What is the plural form of the following words?

piano	memo	video
taco	photo	radio

2. Other words ending in **o** add **-es** when forming the plural. Write the plural form of <u>potato</u>, <u>tomato</u>, <u>echo</u>, and <u>hero</u>.

3. When words end in **s**, **ch**, **sh**, or **x**, the plural is formed by adding **-es**. Make these words plural: <u>speech</u>, <u>reflex</u>, <u>sandwich</u>, <u>brush</u>, and <u>circus</u>.

Word Pattern

To form the plural of most nouns, add **-s**. To form the plural of nouns ending with **s**, **sh**, **ch**, and **x**, add **-es**. Nouns ending in **o** sometimes form the plural by adding either **-s** or **-es**.

equently misspelled word

1. Sort these plural list words into two columns. Title one column "Base Word + **-s**" and the other "Base Word + **-es**."

echoes	matches	tomatoes	capsules	mosquitoes
audiences	vegetables	refugees	heroes	scratches

2. A dictionary can help you find the plural form of a word. Locate the entry for the singular, then look at the end of the entry. Notice the sample below:

> **cri•sis** (krī´sis) **1** the turning point in a serious illness, after which it is known whether the patient is expected to live or die. **2** an important or deciding event. **3** a time or state of danger or anxious waiting. *The British people faced a crisis during the Battle of Britain.* *n., pl.* **cri•ses** (-sēz).

a) Use a dictionary to find the plural forms of the following nouns: child, phenomenon, hypothesis.

b) Find the singular form of these plural nouns: **data**, **women**, **halves**.

3. Some of the list words have unusual vowel combinations. Complete each word with the correct vowels. Then circle, colour, or highlight these letters.

a) mosq_ _toes **b)** m_ _nt_ _ns **c)** veg_tables

d) capt_ _n **e)** refug_ _s

4. The word capsule has many meanings. Write a sentence for each of the following meanings:

a) space capsule **b)** capsule used in medicine

c) time capsule **d)** a capsule comment

SPELLING SECRETS

Remember that **all right** is two words by thinking of its opposite, *all wrong*.

Writing and Revising

1. a) Create a cartoon or comic strip for one or more of these captions:

- Dams rush in where beavers fear to swim.
- You can't reach an old dog with two sticks.
- A little leaning is a dangerous thing.
- The burly bird squishes the worm.

b) Choose a photograph or cartoon and make up your own caption for it. (Hint: You might use one of the cartoons in this book.)

2. The plural form of <u>potato</u> isn't the only word that is easy to misspell. Here are some other words ending in **o**. Use their plural form in a sentence. (Hint: A dictionary will give you the correct plural spelling.)

    a) logo   **b)** rodeo   **c)** yo-yo

    d) so-and-so   **e)** soprano   **f)** solo

3. Use the plural form of the underlined words to rewrite these comic strip captions.

a) I tell you there were two <u>hoax</u>!

b) IMPOSSIBLE! THE <u>SKI</u> WERE KEPT IN <u>BOX</u> UNDER THE STAIRS!

c) Then did the <u>picture</u> we saw come from the <u>video</u>?

d) No! And neither did those <u>clown</u> work for travelling <u>circus</u>!

e) Well, your <u>guess</u> are not going to solve these <u>case</u>!

LANGUAGE MATTERS

- Comic cartoons have been making people laugh for over 2000 years, ever since Roman times.
- The comics of the 1600s and 1700s in Europe were often used to inform people of religious and political injustices.
- By the 1800s, comic strips (a series of drawings that tell a story) were published as small booklets.
- Speech balloons were used in the first all-colour comic strips back in 1893 in New York City.

The Editing Desk

Capital Letters There are many rules for using capital letters. Here are some of the most common ones. Use capital letters for

- proper nouns.
- the initials of people's names.
- the first word of a sentence.
- the pronoun "I."
- acronyms and some abbreviations that use initials.
- names of languages, nationalities, and religions.

The following excerpt from Roch Carrier's short story "The Hockey Sweater" shows several uses of capital letters.

❝ That day I had one of the greatest disappointments of my life! I would even say that on that day I experienced a very great sorrow. Instead of the red, white, and blue Montreal Canadiens sweater, Monsieur Eaton had sent us a blue and white sweater with a maple leaf on the front— the sweater of the Toronto Maple Leafs. ❞

1. Many English last names (always capitalized) come from the name of a trade or occupation (only capitalized at the beginning of a sentence). Can you match these names with the correct trade?

Surname	Trade
1. Mason	a) doorkeeper
2. Thatcher	b) barrel maker
3. Porter	c) carpenter
4. Keeler	d) potter
5. Crocker	e) bricklayer
6. Cooper	f) roofer
7. Sawyer	g) barge worker

2. For each of these categories, write five words that would have to be capitalized. For a category such as "mountains," you might list *Mount Robson*, *Mount McKinley*, *Mount Everest*, and so on.

    a) languages   **b)** cities   **c)** oceans

    d) countries   **e)** lakes or rivers

3. Anagrams is a game of re-arranging the letters of a word to make other words. Curiously, many first names (always capitalized) are anagrams for other names. For example, the letters in *Jean* can be re-arranged to make *Jane*. *Tania* becomes *Anita*. How many other first names can you find below? (The number of anagram names is given in parentheses.)

    a) Clara (1)   **b)** Carol (2)   **c)** Ronald (2)   **d)** Leandre (3)

14 Doubling Consonants

Happy Birthday

to a good friend who's

funny
full of energy
attractive
SUCCESSFUL
beginning a new year
A WINNER
setting the pace

Notice how many of the words on the card have double consonants.

battery
bubble
committed
equipped
fallen
horror
mirror
occurred
offered
omitted
ordered
ripped
success
trapped
travelling

OTHER PATTERNS
deposit
digit
*happened
limit
*until

Thinking about Words

1. Sometimes double consonants are part of the base word. Rewrite these words, circling the double consonants: <u>attractive</u>, <u>full</u>, <u>successful</u>, <u>happy</u>.

2. Write the base word in each of the following: <u>funny</u>, <u>winner</u>, <u>setting</u>. Each word is only one syllable and ends in a short vowel and a consonant. What happens to these base words when the ending is added? (Notice that the endings begin with a vowel.)

3. The base word <u>begin</u> also ends in a short vowel and a consonant. Say the word aloud. Which syllable is stressed?

Now look at the word <u>beginning</u>. What happens when **-ing** is added to the base? If the stress is on the last syllable in a two-syllable word that ends in a vowel and a consonant, the consonant is usually doubled when adding endings beginning with a vowel. What list words fit this pattern?

Word Pattern

When a base word ends in a short vowel and a consonant, double the final consonant when adding endings such as **-ed** and **-ing**. Example: step + ed = ste<u>pp</u>ed

If a base word consists of more than one syllable, the same doubling rule applies *if* the stress is on the final syllable. Example: regret + ing = regre<u>tt</u>ing

SPELLING SECRETS

Notice that full as a base word has a double consonant (as in fully), but when it is a suffix it has only one l (as in successful).

1. The list words below all contain double consonants. Complete the words and highlight the double consonants.

a) ba_ _ery   **b)** bu_ _le   **c)** fa_ _en

d) ho_ _or   **e)** mi_ _or   **f)** o_ _ered

g) su_ _e_ _   **h)** ha_ _ened   **i)** co_ _itted

2. These list words have double consonants as a result of adding **-ed** or **-ing** to the base. Rewrite each word followed by its base word.

a) trapped   **b)** ripped   **c)** committed

d) equipped   **e)** occurred   **f)** omitted

3. Add **-ed**, **-or**, or **-ing** to the following base words. You will need to decide whether the consonant should be doubled. What rule determines this?

a) control + ed = _____   **b)** offer + ing = _____

c) regret + ed = _____   **d)** propel + er = _____

e) order + ing = _____   **f)** happen + ing = _____

g) commit + ed = _____

4. You have probably heard the familiar cheerleading cry, "S-U-C-C-E-S-S. That's the way to spell success!" Information that is communicated in the form of music or rhythm is sometimes easier to remember.

Try creating cheers or rhythms to help you remember the spelling of some list words. You might be able to use the same chant for **digit**, **limit**, and **until** since they all have five letters.

Writing and Revising

1. Use the double-consonant words in the birthday card on page 57 to create your own greeting card. If possible, use publishing software and a printer to give a more professional look to your card.

2. Use as many of the list words as you can to write a greeting card for two of the following situations:

- male birthday
- bon voyage
- female birthday
- belated birthday
- get well soon
- seasonal holiday greeting

3. Rewrite the passage below and correct the spelling mistakes. (Hint: All the incorrect words have something to do with double consonants.)

> It was the ocasion of my friend's birthday. The sun was softly shimering on the lake. The day was going to be a succes. I just knew it! My sugestion was to throw a great party. Melissa wasn't having any of that. Stuborn doesn't begin to describe her. She realy can be a surrprising pain. Still, we found enough to ocuppy our time, and the day wasn't a totall los. But I certainlly don't reccomend a birthday without having a diner party!

4. Why do you think **until** ends in only one **l**? Many words that end in an /l/ sound double the **l**. Can you list ten examples?

The Editing Desk

Why is the final t in commit not doubled in commitment? Because the ending **-ment** begins with a consonant, not a vowel.

What Is a Verb? Verbs tell a reader what action or state of being is happening in a sentence.

Action Verbs: tell what the subject of the sentence is doing. In the sentence, "The candle glowed in the darkness," glowed is an action verb.

Linking Verbs: link or connect the subject to a word that describes the subject. In the sentence, "Too many mosquitoes are outside my tent" are is a linking verb. The most common linking verb is **to be**. Its forms are *am, is, are, was, were, be, been,* and *being.*

Notice the action verbs (underlined) and the linking verbs (double underlined) in this passage from Robert Mason Lee's novel *Death and Deliverance*. (Hint: A "Labrador" is a helicopter used by Canadian search-and-rescue teams.)

❝ The Labrador's engines <u>are</u> <u>shielded</u> by metal screens on the forward inlets, about the same gauge as that <u>used</u> on car head lamps. The screens <u>prevent</u> foreign objects from fouling the turbines, but they <u>are</u> not <u>heated</u>, and they <u>gather</u> ice as a net <u>gathers</u> fish. ❞

1. Choose a piece of your own writing and highlight the verbs.

2. As shown in this chart, other forms of verbs can be created by adding endings to base words.

Base Word	Ending	List Word
order	-ed	ordered
trap	-ed	trapped
travel	-ing	travelling

a) Write the base words for the following verbs:

calculating	**equipped**	**occurred**
committed	**fallen**	referred
continuing	forgotten	skiing

b) Write a paragraph on any subject. Include at least four of the base verbs from part (a) in your paragraph.

3. a) Find examples of verbs in advertisements that you think are effective.

b) Explain in a paragraph how the effective use of verbs can motivate people to buy products.

LANGUAGE MATTERS

A very common verb used in writing stories is <u>said</u>. While there is nothing wrong with using this action word, it doesn't give the reader much of a picture of the speaker. Here are some other verbs that can be used in place of *said*:

blurted	moaned	sighed
cackled	questioned	slurred
giggled	shrieked	snapped

15 Dropping the Final e

Notice how many words in the announcement have the ending **-ed** or **-ing**. In some cases, it's just a matter of adding these letters to the end of the base word. At other times, letters must be dropped or added to the base word before adding the ending.

Announcing!

Grand Opening of

AL'S VIDEO SHOP

HELP!

We've created a monster. We've just received 300 new video games. They're taking over our store! Exciting specials every day.

We're located at the corner of Appleby and New Street. Hoping to see you soon.

admiring
arrival
celebrating
convincing
cyclist
dancing
exciting
icy
noisy
separating
shining
solving
stylish
university
wavy

OTHER PATTERNS

chalet
*could
*either
initials
politicians

Thinking about Words

1. Write the base word for each of these words taken from the announcement: announcing, created, received, taking, **exciting**, located, hoping.

What does each of the base words have in common? What, if any, changes were made to each base word before the suffix was added?

2. Notice that each base word in the previous activity ends in an **e** and that each ending begins with a vowel. When an ending beginning with a consonant is added to a base word ending in **e**, is the final **e** still dropped? Examine these words:

announce	hope	excite
announced	hoped	excited
announcing	hoping	**exciting**
announcement	hopeful	excitement

Word Pattern

Generally, when a base word ends in a silent **e**, you
- drop the final **e** when adding an ending beginning with a vowel (**-ed**, **-ing**, **-y**).
- do not drop the final **e** when the ending begins with a consonant (**-ment**, **-ly**, **-ful**).

Working with Words

1. Review the list words. Notice that the final **e** was dropped from many of these words before the ending was added.

    a) Write the base word for each of the following list words:

        admiring   separating

        celebrating   shining

        convincing   solving

        dancing

    b) Add **-ing** to these base words:

        skate   locate   freeze

        produce   compete   propose

2. Add **y** to the end of the following base words.

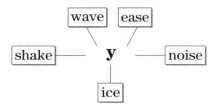

3. Unscramble the syllables in the box to form three list words:

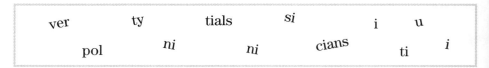

Writing and Revising

1. Collect at least ten print advertisements announcing something about a business or product. Choose one that you think is the most interesting and effective. Use it as a model to rewrite Al's Video Shop announcement (p. 61).

2. **a)** A **chalet** is a style of house. Do you know what it looks like? Match the following house styles with the correct description.

1. bungalow	**a)** small, roughly built house
2. cabin	**b)** large, stately house
3. chalet	**c)** attached houses, two or more storeys tall
4. cottage	**d)** one-storey house
5. mansion	**e)** a house with wide, overhanging eaves
6. townhouse	**f)** a small, often uninsulated house

b) Design a bedroom or media room. You might consider a futuristic style. Attach illustrations or photographs of interior decorating styles you particularly like.

3. Identify all the list words that are misspelled in this adjective poem and write them correctly.

Stars twinkling in the night sky
Dansing, celebrateing, shineing
Seperating the blackness like icey crystals
Convinsing us to gaze upward
We pass the time admireing their beauty
Until the arrival of the sun
Masks their sparkling light.

The Editing Desk

Verbs: Present Tense   There are three basic types of verb tenses: present, past, and future. Present-tense verbs have different forms for singular and plural subjects.

Present Tense: Subject and Verb Forms				
I	**he/she/it**	**you**	**we**	**they**
I travel.	He travels.	You travel.	We travel.	They travel.
—	She travels.	—	Sean and I travel.	Sean and Marika travel.
—	It travels.	—		

Notice that the only change in the verb is the **-s** ending for the *he*, *she*, and *it* subject forms.

The same rules apply for adding **-s** to verbs as they do for making plurals. The chart below summarizes these rules:

Present Tense: Verb Endings		
Normal Pattern: add -s	**Words Ending in s, sh, or ch: add -es**	**Words Ending in y: drop the y + add -ies**
travel + s = travels	pass + s = passes wish + s = wishes catch + s = catches	fly + s = flies

This passage from Susan Forest's novel *The Dragon Prince* shows the use of verbs in the present tense (underlined).

❝ Erlyn <u>takes</u> her hand and <u>leads</u> her into a large building of white stone that <u>is</u> smooth as ceramic. The floors <u>are</u> polished, inlaid wood. He <u>takes</u> her through several hallways to a sunny room with a wall of high windows. ❞

1. Rewrite the following sentences, inserting the present tense of the verb shown in parentheses.

   a) Rumours _____ faster than a jet aircraft. (to travel)

   b) One chance remark _____ innocent enough. (to seem)

   c) Then one person _____ another, and others _____ it to more people. (to tell), (to explain)

   d) The next thing you _____, everyone _____ their version is what happened. (to know), (to think)

   e) No one _____ to find out the *real* story. (to try)

2. Add **-s** or **-es** to the following verbs and then use each verb in a sentence.

a) blush	**b)** crackle	**c)** dilute
d) hurry	**e)** rescue	**f)** pour
g) match	**h)** crash	**i)** rely

LANGUAGE MATTERS

Words containing the letter **x** are not common in the English language. Use a dictionary to find the meaning of these **eXciting** words:

- lexicon
- matrix
- vex
- xylem
- xenophobia
- pixel
- orthodox
- xerography

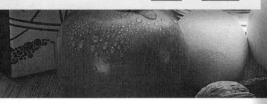

Adding Endings y to i

Canada's Food Guide

Grain Products	Energy = Calories
5–12 servings	If you follow Canada's Food Guide, you will get between 1800 and 3200 Calories each day. Foods such as candies, cookies, and pastries are high in refined sugar and contain "empty" calories. To maintain a healthy diet, choose a variety of foods from the four food groups.
Vegetables and Fruit 5–10 servings	
Milk Products 3–4 servings	
Meat and Alternatives 2–3 servings	

Candies and pastries have something in common other than empty **calories**! How does their pattern for forming the plural differ from words such as foods or groups?

batteries
berries
calories
cities
families
groceries
hurried
implied
memories
notified
qualified
satisfied
studied
tries
worried

OTHER PATTERNS

diamond
marriage
parliament
*schedule
*scholar

Thinking about Words

1. Write the singular form of these words taken from the class display on healthy eating: candies, pastries. Notice that both base words end in a consonant + y, unlike calories whose singular form is calorie not calory.

2. In almost all cases, when a suffix is added to a base word ending in a consonant + y, the **y** changes to **i**. For example:

$$try + ed = tried$$
$$pity + ful = pitiful$$
$$deny + al = denial$$

The exception to this rule occurs with the suffix **-ing**. Try changing the **y** to **i** in fly + ing. Why do you think the **y** stays the same? Complete the following word equations:

a) occupy + ing = _____   **b)** fancy + ful = _____

c) classify + ed = _____   **d)** photocopy + ing = _____

e) reply + ed = _____   **f)** bury + al = _____

Word Pattern

When adding a suffix other than **-ing** to a base word ending in a consonant + y, change the **y** to **i**.

equently misspelled word

1. Change the verbs in parentheses to the past tense by adding **-ed**.

   a) I (hurry) home because I was (worry) about my brother. I had (try) to call him earlier but got no answer.

   b) Jasmine (study) hard for her driver's test and (qualify) for her beginner's licence. Her instructor was (satisfy) with her driving and (notify) the examiner that she was ready for a road test.

2. How many words can you form from the base word <u>memory</u>? Try to build at least five words. A dictionary may help.

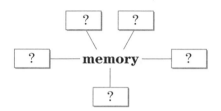

3. **a)** Supply the double consonants for each list word below. Highlight the double consonants in some way.

   be_ _ies   hu_ _ied   ba_ _eries   wo_ _ied

   b) Fill in the vowel combinations in these words. How might you remember these vowels?

   d_ _mond   marr_ _ge   parl_ _ment

4. Change each of the nouns in parentheses to the plural form.

   a) (Battery) not included.   **b)** (Memory) are made of this!

   c) (Supply) are limited.   **d)** (Family) welcome.

   e) Helps prevent (cavity).   **f)** Colour (copy) $2.00 each.

1. **a)** Plan a day's menu that follows the recommendations listed in the food guide on page 65. Redesign that display to include your menu plan.

   b) Write a paragraph agreeing or disagreeing with this statement: It is possible to maintain a balanced diet by eating in fast-food restaurants.

LANGUAGE MATTERS

Calories are units which measure energy.

- 1 boiled egg = 80 calories
- 1 medium apple = 117 calories
- 10 French fries = 155 calories
- chocolate cake (5 cm²) = 356 calories

---

2. **a)** Each of the following topics is based on a different list word. Can you guess which list word inspired each topic?

   - storing electrical energy
   - types of governments
   - modern supermarket
   - precious gemstones
   - dieting
   - suburbs

   b) Choose one of the topics from part (a) or make up one of your own. Research an aspect of the topic and create a one-page display similar to this model:

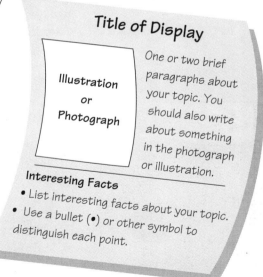

Title of Display

Illustration or Photograph

One or two brief paragraphs about your topic. You should also write about something in the photograph or illustration.

Interesting Facts
- List interesting facts about your topic.
- Use a bullet (•) or other symbol to distinguish each point.

3. The letters **sch** in **schedule** and **scholar** are pronounced /sk/. Write four more words for this sound pattern, then use each word in a sentence. (Hint: A dictionary will help you find your words.)

Verbs: Past Tense Verbs in the past tense describe an action that happens *before* the present. Most fiction and non-fiction writing is in the past tense. The usual ending for a verb in the past tense is **-ed**. Compare the following sentences:

- Tanya play**s** soccer on Tuesday. (present tense)
- Tanya play**ed** soccer last Tuesday. (past tense)

The linking verb **to be** is an exception to this rule.

Present Tense	Past Tense
I am.	—
He/She/It is.	I/He/She/It was.
You/We/They are.	You/We/They were.

The past-tense verbs have been underlined in this passage from Sharon Siamon's novel *Ski for Your Mountain*.

66 Every wall and window pane <u>was</u> blackened and streaked with smoke and soot. The whole place <u>smelled</u> terrible; the stale smoke smell <u>was</u> deep into carpets and curtains and furniture. Even the cold cereal they <u>tried</u> to eat for breakfast <u>tasted</u> smoky! 99

1. Use the past tense of the verbs in parentheses to complete these sentences.

    a) The women _____ into the room. (to walk)

    b) Matches _____ never kept on the counter. (to be)

    c) They _____ two mountains in one week. (to climb)

    d) It _____ only last week that he _____ his friend in the hospital. (to be), (to visit)

2. Rewrite the following paragraph by changing the underlined verbs to the past tense.

It <u>is</u> past midnight and I <u>am</u> downtown at a phone booth. My friends <u>are</u> supposed to pick me up at eleven but they <u>are</u> late. I <u>count</u> the change in my pocket. Not enough. I <u>wonder</u> how to call my parents. The last time I <u>call</u> collect, my dad <u>asks</u> me if I <u>spend</u> all my telephone money. I <u>pick</u> up the phone and <u>press</u> 0.

Did you notice some "bloopers" in this note? When one word is accidentally used in place of another, the result can be quite entertaining. What corrections does Mr. Leighter need to make to his note?

Dear Teacher:

Jason has missed school for the past seven days because he's really sick with chicken pogs, an inspected toenail, and strip throat. The doctor says he will probably be home for another week. Please send homework with one of his friends

Thank the class for the get-well card. Jason certainly enjoyed it.

Sincerely,
Mrs. C. M. Leighter

absolutely
actually
approximately
certainly
especially
eventually
generally
happily
quietly
really
safely
silently
surely
terribly
usually

OTHER PATTERNS

debt
doubt
*eighty
*excellent
often

Thinking about Words

1. Four words in the note to the teacher end in the suffix **-ly**. Find these words and beside each one write its base word.

2. Notice that in the case of <u>really</u>, <u>certainly</u>, and <u>sincerely</u>, **-ly** has been added with no change to the base word. What has happened to the base word in <u>probably</u>? What letters were dropped and why? Write the word as it would look if the ending had simply been added to the base. Does it look strange to you? How would you pronounce this word?

Word Pattern

• The suffix **-ly** is usually added to base words without changing the spelling of the base. For example, <u>quiet</u> becomes **quietly**. Notice, however, that a double **l** is formed when **-ly** is added to a base word that ends in **l**. For example, <u>eventual</u> becomes **eventually**.

• In the case of words ending in **-le**, the **le** is dropped before the suffix is added. For example, <u>terrible</u> becomes **terribly**.

• In words ending in consonant + y, the **y** changes to **i** before the suffix is added. For example, <u>happy</u> becomes **happily**.

*frequently misspelled word

1. Write each of the following list words in the form of an equation.
Example: finally = final + ly

    a) actually   **b)** usually   **c)** really

    d) generally   **e)** eventually   **f)** especially

2. Tom Swifties are puns created by using an adverb in a humorous way, as in "The power has gone off," Astrid said darkly.

   Link the adverbs in the box with the sentences below to make Tom Swifties. Try writing a few of your own!

patiently	absently	boldly
sheepishly	sharply	aimlessly

    a) "I don't like dull pencils!" Estevan complained _____.

    b) "Use a strong typeface," Hamish said _____.

    c) "Will the doctor see me soon?" Nicole asked _____.

    d) "I wasn't trying to hit the target," Malik said _____.

    e) "Yes, I skipped school," Allison answered _____.

    f) "I can't find the lambs," Kevin stated _____.

3. Unscramble the syllables to find list words.

    a) er•ly•al•gen   **b)** pe•cial•es•ly   **c)** tu•ly•ac•al

    d) so•ab•ly•lute   **e)** ly•su•u•al

4. a) Four list words contain silent consonants. Write the list words that match the following shapes, then circle the silent consonants.

b) Link these shapes to four list words that contain double consonants.

1. You can have a lot of fun playing with the meanings and sounds of words. See if you can match the words in the first column with the definitions in the second column. The first one has been done for you.

1. *kidney*	**a)** *your baby brother's (or sister's) knee*
2. paradox	**b)** this dog likes watermelons
3. denial	**c)** a make of car
4. illegal	**d)** two doctors
5. melancholy	**e)** the world's longest river
6. afford	**f)** a sick bird

2. Rewrite the following sentences by substituting a list word for the underlined phrase. (Hint: You may have to re-arrange some words.)

a) The crowd waited <u>without speaking a word</u> while the firefighters fought the blaze.

b) Everyone was <u>in a most extreme manner</u> frightened, <u>in particular</u> the family members of the victims.

c) It wasn't until the blaze was out, and all the victims were rescued <u>free from harm or danger</u>, that everyone cheered <u>with joy and gladness</u>.

d) The fire caused <u>very near but not over</u> $400 000 damage.

3. We can thank the classical languages of Latin and ancient Greek for some of the unusual spellings of English words. The word **debt** was spelled *dette* until scholars decided it should be spelled more like its Latin equivalent *debitum*. The word **doubt** came from the Latin *dubitare*, but was first spelled *doute*. Can you guess how these Latin words are currently spelled?

Latin Word	Original English Spelling	Current English Spelling
recepta	receite	
exemplum	essample	
anchora	ancor	
lingua	langage	
adventura	aventure	

Verbs: Future Tense Actions that take place beyond the present time require the use of future-tense verbs. This tense is made up of **will** plus the verb. Notice how, in this example, the spelling of the verb is the same for each subject:

I *will talk* to Roberta tomorrow.   You *will talk* to Roberta tomorrow.
She *will talk* to Roberta tomorrow.   They *will talk* to Roberta tomorrow.

This passage from "A Car with a Mind of Its Own" was written by Andrew Revkin in 1988 concerning cars in the year 2001. The future tense has been underlined.

66 The biggest change in the car of 2001 <u>will be</u> under the hood, in the electronics. Most cars <u>will have</u> a powerful integrated electronic nervous system and central brain that <u>will do</u> everything.... 99

1. Choose a future-tense form of the verb in parentheses.

   a) There _____ two adults to supervise. (to be)

   b) The audience _____ by the back door. (to enter)

   c) You _____ tomatoes and corn for the recipe. (to need)

   d) Everyone _____ to buy a ticket to next month's concert. (to want)

2. Choose five adverbs from the unit list and use each in a sentence with a future-tense verb. For example, "I absolutely will not go with you to the mall!"

3. The future tense is sometimes used in advertisements to persuade people to act before it is too late.

Bug-Away Repellent

Free Samples

This offer will definitely end soon! And so will your bug problems.

Write an advertisement for a product. Use the future tense to urge people to *buy now*.

Review
Units 13-17

Working with Words

1. For each of the following sentences, add **-ed** or **-ing** to the base words in parentheses.

    a) After I (commit) two faults, I was (worry) I would never make the jump. Luckily, I (qualify) for the finals on my last try.

    b) When we were (travel) to Fredericton, we saw a bad car accident that had (occur) just a short time before. Three people were (trap) in the car, but a rescue truck (equip) with the Jaws of Life (rip) the doors off of the vehicle. The rescue workers (hurry) to get the people out and then (carry) them to safety.

2. Which one of the sets of double consonants completes the list words that follow? (Hint: You may use the same set more than once.)

ff	ss	bb	pp
ll	rr	tt	cc

    a) exce_ _ent   **b)** de_ _erts   **c)** su_ _e_ _   **d)** hu_ ied

    e) ha_ _ened   **f)** te_ _ibly   **g)** o_ _ered   **h)** bu_ _le

    i) ho_ _or   **j)** ba_ _ery   **k)** wo_ _ied   **l)** be_ _ies

3. Write the plural form of each of the following words. (Hint: The plural forms are among the list words in Units 13–17.)

    a) potato   **b)** family   **c)** match

    d) datum   **e)** memory   **f)** tomato

    g) woman   **h)** half   **i)** hero

4. Add the ending **-ly** to each of the following words:

    a) happy + ly = _____   **b)** eventual + ly = _____

    c) general + ly = _____   **d)** certain + ly = _____

    e) terrible + ly = _____   **f)** usual + ly = _____

5. The missing letters in these words are letters that cannot be remembered by simply sounding out the word. They may be schwa vowels, silent letters, and so forth. Complete each word, then highlight these tricky letters in some way.

a) di_m_nd   **b)** marr_ _ge   **c)** parl_ _ment

d) ex_ell_nt   **e)** of_en   **f)** dou_t

g) de_t   **h)** s_ _edule   **i)** s_ _olar

Proofreading

Rewrite the paragraph below, correcting all the misspelled words.

> My friend and I decided to make a casserole and some deserts for a fund-raiser at school. First we went to the store to buy grocries. We studied the list: potatos, berrys, tomatos, sugar, milk. We huried because it was nearly closing time. The clerk offerred to pack our bags, but I said "No, thanks! We're two very capable woman." As we left the store, I heard a thud. To my horor I saw that the milk had riped through the bag and spilled all over the floor! I was realy quiet as we helped to clean up the mess.

Dictionary Skills

Inflected Forms How do you find out how to spell a word such as *mosquitoes*? There is no separate dictionary entry for the plural form of most nouns. Neither is there a separate dictionary entry for verbs to which **-ed** or **-ing** have been added, nor for adverbs which have been formed by adding **-ly** to a base word.

The correct spelling of these forms is usually found at the end of the dictionary entry for the singular form of nouns and the present tense of verbs. Examine this entry:

> **mos•qui•to** (mə skē´tō)   a small, slender insect: *The female mosquito can pierce the skin of people and animals and draw blood, causing a sting that itches.*   *n., pl.* **mosqui•toes** or **mos•qui•tos**.

At the end of the entry is the information *n., pl.* **mosqui•toes** or **mos•qui•tos**. This means that the plural form of the noun (*n., pl.*) can be spelled either with an **-es** or **-s** ending. The fact that *mosquitoes* comes first suggests that this spelling of the plural form is generally preferred in most parts of Canada.

SPELLING SECRETS

· · · · · · ·

Some dictionaries do not list inflected forms if the endings can be added to the root word without any change in spelling.

Answer the following questions by locating the entry word in the dictionary and using the information at the end of the entry.

1. How is the past tense of the verb <u>omit</u> spelled? What happens when **-ing** is added to the verb?

2. a) Which is correct, *Snow White and the Seven Dwarfs* or *Snow White and the Seven Dwarves*?

b) Why is the spelling of the hockey team The Toronto Maple Leafs unusual?

3. Only one of the following words is spelled correctly. Which one is it?

ocassionally
occasionaly
occassionally
occasionally

Language Power

Writers sometimes use *buzz words* or *jargon* to explain a point. If the reader happens to understand the jargon, communication may be effective. Too often, however, buzz words just get in the way of understanding. Consider the following statement: "Hanif could maximize his potential through attention to completion dates and assignment requirements."

What does this mean in plain English? It means "Hanif could do better if he did his assignments properly and on time."

Link each phrase in the column on the left with its "plain English" version in the column on the right.

Buzz Words	Plain English
1. shows disregard for the ownership rights of others	**a)** talks back
2. cannot control physical aggression	**b)** doesn't listen
3. has difficulty with computational skills	**c)** has a messy locker
4. needs to focus attention on the speaker	**d)** steals
5. should develop organization skills for personal property	**e)** hits others
6. challenges the authority of the teacher	**f)** can't count

Writing and Revising

1. Choose two of the following list words and use them to write a caption for a cartoon. Describe or draw the cartoon.

mosquitoes	bubble	either	diamond	really
all right	ripped	icy	calories	eighty

2. Match each clue to the correct list word.

1. reflect on this
2. cars and TV remotes need these to work
3. after-dinner treat, not a hot climate!
4. what you might be doing with your face in part (c).
5. B.C. and Alberta have high ones; P.E.I. has none
6. exercise is what this person gets
7. with this word, something is left out
8. the hardest stone on earth

a) dessert
b) mountains
c) mirror
d) cyclist
e) diamond
f) batteries
g) admiring (it)
h) omitted

3. a) Use some of the list words below to complete the Grand Opening announcement. (Hint: Not all of the words will be used.)

absolutely	exciting	noisy	satisfied
calories	groceries	often	separating
committed	matches	qualified	stylish
dancing	memories	quietly	vegetables

b) Create your own unusual business announcement. Use as many list words from Units 13–17 as you can.

GRAND OPENING

Stuff-It-In-Your-Face Café

There's a new, _____, fast-food eatery in your neighbourhood. Forget about shopping for the _____ on your list. Forget healthy eating and all those good-for-you _____. Say hello to the high _____ you get from gooey, greasy foods. Here's a _____ restaurant that will bring back pleasant _____ of times spent _____ eating in a calm atmosphere.

You and your friends can eat until you're _____ full. Then, spend a while _____ to some _____ new music provided by our _____ disc jockey. At Stuff-It-In-Your-Face, we're _____ to making sure our customers are _____.

1. Some capital letters are missing from the story below. Rewrite the passage and correct the errors.

spring-break disasters

it was supposed to be a holiday. that's what my brother raj—or rj as we call him—said. we were to go up to our place on little lake about an hour's drive north of winnipeg. i only have myself to blame, i guess, since i agreed to go. i mean, spring break isn't summer; it's still the middle of winter here!

well, we packed up friday night and left early saturday. naturally it was snowing. the traffic reports on the cbc didn't sound good, but rj only laughed them off. i remember laughing, too. stupid me! we ended up in a snowdrift after we turned off highway 84. the good thing was we had a car phone. the bad thing was we spent all day trying to keep warm while waiting for the caa truck to arrive.

what a disaster!

2. Write a sentence for each of the following verbs. The tense you should use is shown in parentheses.

a) worry (past tense)
b) separate (future tense)
c) echo (present tense)
d) arrive (future tense)
e) omit (past tense)
f) hurry (present tense)

3. Adding **-ed** and **-ing** to verbs sometimes requires a change in the spelling of the base word. Complete these verb equations.

a) rely + ed = _____
b) trap + ing = _____
c) slam + ed = _____
d) magnify + ed = _____
e) blur + ing = _____
f) regret + ed = _____
g) occur + ed = _____
h) happen + ing = _____

4. Rewrite the sentences below using the correct form of the verb listed in parentheses.

a) Last Saturday, Naomi, Kyle, and I _____ down Centre Street to catch the bus. (to walk, future tense)

b) We _____ to meet everyone at the mall. (to want, past tense)

c) Anyway, when the bus _____ the corner, we _____ on. (to turn, past tense), (to jump, past tense)

d) But it _____ the 85B bus, not the 89. (to be, past tense)

e) By the time we _____ our mistake, we _____ ten blocks out of our way. (to realize, past tense), (to be, past tense)

1. Each of these items comes from the name or nickname of a real person. Try to figure out as many as you can. (Hint: Use a dictionary or encyclopedia if you get stuck.)

- **a)** teddy bear
- **b)** pasteurize
- **c)** diesel
- **d)** maverick
- **e)** derrick
- **f)** silhouette

2. Compound words are two words that have been joined together to create a new word. The new word is related to both the smaller words (see Unit 10); for example, <u>sidewalk</u>, <u>overpass</u>, and <u>downtown</u>. See if you can complete these sets of compound words by providing the missing smaller word. The first one has been done for you.

- **a)** base / foot / basket + *ball*
- **b)** back / fore / under + _____
- **c)** bank / cook / text + _____
- **d)** blue / goose / straw + _____
- **e)** day / flash / high + _____
- **f)** high / sub / drive + _____

3. An anagram is a word or a phrase that is formed by re-arranging letters of another word or phrase. The word *sit*, for example, can be rewritten as *its*.

Each of the following words is an anagram of a girl's name. Can you figure them out?

- **a)** gem = _____
- **b)** teak = _____
- **c)** gain = _____
- **d)** hurt = _____
- **e)** sail = _____
- **f)** issue = _____

Concepts of Prefixes and Suffixes

Although these safety rules are simple, some of the words are complex. They involve adding either prefixes or suffixes to a base word or a root word. These additions often change the meaning of the base word or alter its part of speech.

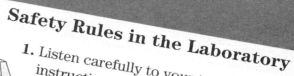
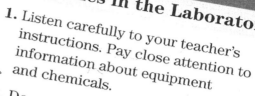

Safety Rules in the Laboratory

1. Listen carefully to your teacher's instructions. Pay close attention to information about equipment and chemicals.

2. Do not leave your experiment unattended.

3. Help prevent accidents by keeping your work area uncluttered.

4. Do not interfere with the work of others.

amusement
astronaut
attendance
autograph
automatic
confidence
doubtful
enjoyment
experience
insurance
interfere
interview
prediction
prevent
successful

OTHER PATTERNS
*budget
occupation
profession
*referee
vocation

Thinking about Words

1. What is the base of the word <u>carefully</u>? Notice that two suffixes have been added to the base. Complete this word equation:

$$\underline{\hspace{2cm}} + \underline{\hspace{2cm}} + \underline{\hspace{2cm}} = \text{carefully}$$
$$\text{base word} \qquad \text{suffix} \qquad \text{suffix}$$

2. The prefixes **un-** and **inter-** each carry a meaning which affects the base or root word. **Un-** means "not" and **inter-** often means "between" or "among." How do these meanings apply to the words <u>uncluttered</u> and <u>interfere</u>?

3. Sometimes a letter is dropped from the base word when a suffix is added. What letter is dropped from the base <u>attend</u> in the word <u>attention</u>?
   Try to say attend + tion. Can you suggest why the **d** is dropped?

Word Pattern

Prefixes and suffixes are sometimes added to base words. This addition often changes the meaning or grammatical function of the base word.

1. When you know the meaning of prefixes, root words, and suffixes, it is often easier to figure out the meaning of some very long words. Use the chart below to write a definition for the following words: **astronaut**, <u>autobiography</u>, <u>transportation</u>.

Prefixes	astro- auto- trans-	star, planet, or heavenly body self; same across, over, down, or beyond
Roots	bio port	life to carry
Suffixes	-graph -naut	drawn or written sail

2. Rewrite each list word and include the missing double consonants. Circle the double consonants or highlight them in a different colour.

    a) profe_ _ion **b)** o_ _upation **c)** a_ _endance **d)** su_ _e_ _ful

3. Write as many words as possible using the prefix **inter-**. Score one point for each word.

    Score: 5 = good work;   10 = excellent;   15 = awesome!

4. The **dg** spelling of the sound /j/, as in **budget**, is found in many words. Complete the puzzle below:

    a) a type of homemade candy   _ _dge
    b) courtroom official   _ _dge
    c) small bushes surrounding a lawn   _ _dge
    d) a promise; oath   _ _ _dge
    e) roadway across a river   _ _ _dge

5. The sound /əns/, as in <u>audience</u> and <u>defiance</u>, is usually spelled either **-ence** or **-ance**. Rewrite each of these list words and insert the correct vowel:

    a) attend_nce
    b) confid_nce
    c) experi_nce
    d) insur_nce

SPELLING SECRETS

Remember the "i" in **confidence** by thinking of the base word <u>confide</u>.

1. **a)** List the words in the report sheet below that use prefixes and suffixes.

    b) Underline the prefix or suffix in each word you listed in part (a). Which of these words don't have base words?

EXPERIMENT REPORT SHEET	
Purpose	To identify a liquid by finding its boiling point
Materials	• safety goggles • apron • protective gloves • clear, colourless liquid (supplied by your teacher) • test tube • beaker • thermometer • electric kettle (or other source of boiling water)
Procedure	1. Pour 10 mL of the colourless liquid into the test tube, then place the thermometer in the liquid. 2. Fill the beaker two-thirds full of boiling water. 3. Stand the test tube containing the colourless liquid in this hot water bath. 4. Find the boiling point of the liquid. (Caution: This liquid may be flammable. Keep away from open flame.)
Question	Compare the boiling point of the unknown liquid to your Common Substances chart. What substance do you think the liquid is?

2. It is important to follow laboratory safety rules when you are conducting experiments.

    a) Add at least four more safety rules to those listed on page 79. (Hint: Most science textbooks discuss lab safety.)

    b) Design an experiment report form that includes your rules.

3. Choose five list words that are formed from base words. Write a sentence using both the base word and its changed form. For example, "We had to <u>attend</u> the assembly because the teachers were taking **attendance**."

LANGUAGE MATTERS

If you know what a prefix means, you can often figure out what a word containing that prefix means. Here are some other common prefixes and their definitions:

Prefix	Meaning
anti-	against; the opposite; preventing
post-	after
pre-	before time, place, order, or rank
pro-	forward; in favour of; before

Regular Verb Patterns Regular verbs follow a pattern that is always the same. Here are some regular verb patterns:

- **-s** is added to a verb in the present tense with these forms—*he, she,* or *it.* Example:

    Marlene buy<u>s</u> groceries in the market. (present tense)

- **-ed** is added to a verb to form the past tense. Example:

    The class help<u>ed</u> the new students. (past tense)

1. Complete the sentences by changing the verb form in parentheses to the present tense.

    a) "_____ on down to Kira's Used Bike Lot," the announcer said. (to come)

    b) "Every bike _____ and _____ like a great bargain." (to look), (to feel)

    c) "We _____ deals," the announcer went on, "like Burger Haven _____ food—fast and with lots of zest." (to make), (to cook)

    d) "So if the idea of owning a used bike _____ you excited, Kira _____ she's got the selection you're looking for." (to have), (to say)

2. Record in your notebook all the list words that are verbs. (Hint: Some of the words can be nouns as well as verbs.) Use each word in a sentence. What tenses have you used?

3. Even regular verbs have spelling exceptions. Changing **y** to **i** before adding the ending **-ed** is one. Another exception is dropping the final **e** at the end of a verb before adding the ending. Can you complete these verb equations? (Hint: Not all of the verbs require a change in spelling.)

    a) slam + ed = _____

    b) employ + ed = _____

    c) blame + ed = _____

    d) occupy + ed = _____

    e) knit + ed = _____

    f) copy + ed = _____

20 Contractions

When we communicate with people, whether in written or verbal form, we often use contractions. Reread the interviewer's opening comments aloud, but change the contractions **you're** and <u>what's</u> to their full form. How does this change affect the tone of the interview?

Interview with the Authors

Interviewer: So you're writing a spelling text for Grade 7. What's it like to write a book about spelling?

Scott: It's more difficult than you'd think.

Siamon: You'd better believe it! We're always trying to make a serious topic fun.

Interviewer: Well, we'll let your readers decide whether or not you were successful. Good luck!

aren't
didn't
doesn't
don't
hadn't
it's
let's
that's
there's
they're
they've
we're
wouldn't
you're
you've

OTHER PATTERNS

environment
escape
except
*exercise
*government

Thinking about Words

1. When a contraction is formed, it is often only one letter in the long version that is replaced by the apostrophe. Write the full version of these contractions taken from the interview:

    a) we're   **b)** it's

2. At other times, the apostrophe replaces more than one letter. Write the long form of the contraction <u>we'll</u>.

3. Sometimes the same contraction can represent more than one long form. Write the full version of the contraction <u>you'd</u> as it is used in each of the following sentences:

    a) It's more difficult than you'd think.   **b)** You'd better believe it!

Word Pattern

A contraction is generally a shortened form of two words. One or more letters are removed and replaced by an apostrophe, as in *you are* becoming **you're**.

1. Combine words from the squares to form as many contractions as possible. Choose four contractions from your list to use in sentences. Example: have + not = haven't   They haven't seen us for weeks.

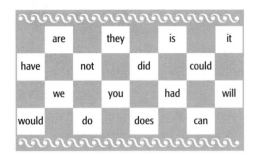

	are		they		is		it
have		not		did		could	
	we		you		had		will
would		do		does		can	

2. Rewrite the following sentences, substituting the underlined words with the correct contraction.

a) Deepak would have gone swimming with his friends if he <u>had not</u> forgotten his bathing suit.

b) "You <u>can not</u> be serious. <u>There is</u> no way <u>I am</u> helping you with your history project."

c) If <u>it is</u> going to rain on Saturday, <u>we will</u> have to postpone the charity car wash.

d) "It <u>does not</u> matter which film <u>we are</u> going to see," Carolyn said, annoyed. "<u>Let us</u> just go to the movies!"

3. Complete each of the following list words:

a) e_er_i_e   **b)** enviro_ _ent   **c)** e_ _ept

d) e_ _ape   **e)** gover_ _ent

1. a) Prepare an interview sheet for one of the following topics (or make up one of your own). Include at least five questions that you can ask in your interview.

- television programs: likes and dislikes
- ways to include bused students in after-school activities
- music likes and dislikes
- qualities of best friends

b) Make a list of any contractions you have used in your interview questions. Circle the contractions that are list words.

2. Write the missing contraction for each of these expressions. Then write what you think each expression means.

   a) _____ sick with worry about her lifeguarding exam.

   b) We _____ care less what you said!

   c) You _____ put a square peg in a round hole.

   d) Attention everyone. _____ get down to business.

   e) Where _____ smoke _____ fire.

   f) My parents want me to get up at 7:00 a.m. on weekends.
   _____ be the day!

3. Contractions are used in informal writing (notes, messages, diaries, and so on) and in speech. The long forms tend to be used in formal writing, such as essays, reports, and business correspondence.

   a) Choose five or more contractions from the unit list and write two different paragraphs that include the words in the following manner:

   • Use the contractions in a paragraph of informal writing.

   • Use the long form of the contractions in a paragraph of formal writing.

   b) Exchange your paragraphs with a classmate and discuss what effect each paragraph had on your partner.

4. At least one **n** in the words **environment** and **government** seems to be silent. Use the following clues to find five words that contain at least one silent letter. When you identify the word, try using it in a sentence.

   a) this person fixes water pipes   _lu_ _e_

   b) very serious; sacred   sol_m_

   c) a building that houses royalty   ca_ _le

   d) a period of one thousand years   mil_e_ _i_m

   e) stringed instrument   g_ _t_r

LANGUAGE MATTERS

One contraction that hasn't been accepted in formal or informal writing is <u>ain't</u>. Originally, *ain't* was a short form for **am not**, but it has also been used incorrectly as a contraction for **to be** and **to have**. Because of this mix-up, and the fact that so many people misuse the word, it's considered a poor choice for writing and speech. There is still no acceptable short form for *am not*.

Verbs: Present Participles The present participle is a verb tense that expresses an action that is happening now. It is formed by combining the present tense of **to be** with the **-ing** form of a verb. In this example, the **-ing** form of *to take* is called the present participle:

I <u>am taking</u> a walk around the block.

1. Choose one of the phone-call situations below (or make up one of your own) and write an imaginary conversation. Use as many forms of am/is/are + the present participle as you can in your dialogue. For example:

The reason I'<u>m calling</u> you is that I'<u>m trying</u> to find out where Sonia <u>is going</u> to school now.

a) you are trying to locate a missing animal

b) you are calling to buy tickets to a concert

c) you are ordering something from a catalogue store

d) you are relaying a message from a friend

2. Another purpose for using **to be** plus the present participle is to express an action that is *continually happening right now*. The present tense, on the other hand, often expresses an action that happens over a period of time but is still happening now.

Present tense: She <u>sits</u> in that chair every day.

Present participle: She <u>is sitting</u> in that chair now.

Write a paragraph based on one of the situations outlined below (or make up your own situation). Include both present-tense and present-participle forms of verbs in your paragraph. (Hint: You might write as if you were explaining your situation to someone else.)

• You are in your favourite restaurant, or doughnut shop, food court, etc., and can't get served.

• A friend (or friends) is late meeting you.

• You are stuck on a bus; the movie you are going to see started five minutes ago.

21 Possessives: Singular

Notice how many of the words in this survey contain apostrophes.

What is the difference between the function of the apostrophe in the word <u>What's</u> versus its function in other words in the survey?

Fitness Survey: What's Your Opinion?

1. Do you think the average teenager's fitness level is higher than the average adult's fitness level? ❑ Yes ❑ No

2. Should the government pay for a portion of a gym's membership fees in order to promote fitness? ❑ Yes ❑ No

3. Do you think a fast-food chain's logo should appear on an athletic event's promotional advertising? ❑ Yes ❑ No

circus's
industry's
journey's
movie's
sandwich's
society's
submarine's
teacher's
teenager's
theatre's
theory's
turtle's
umpire's
victim's
witness's

OTHER PATTERNS

conqueror
creator
elevator
*necessary
*stomach

Thinking about Words

1. The phrase "the average teenager's fitness level" could also be worded "the fitness level of the average teenager." How else could you write the following phrases?

   a) a gym's membership fees

   b) a fast-food chain's logo

   c) an athletic event's promotional advertising

The phrases above are all showing the possessive case.

2. When the base word is singular (meaning just one), the possessive is formed by adding **'s**.

Rewrite all the possessive forms contained in the survey. Underline the base word in each (for example, <u>event</u>'s).

Word Pattern

The possessive form of a noun is mainly used to show ownership. When a noun is singular, add **'s** to the base word to show the possessive case.

1. Correct the underlined possessives in the following sentences by placing an apostrophe in the proper place.

    a) The <u>theatres</u> front door was locked when we first arrived.

    b) The <u>movies</u> crisis occurred when the <u>submarines</u> hatch failed to seal properly.

    c) Do you think it is <u>societys</u> responsibility to protect a <u>victims</u> rights?

    d) Is there an expiry date printed on the <u>sandwichs</u> packaging?

2. Many common expressions contain the possessive form. Match the possessives with the nouns to form ten expressions.

Possessives	Nouns
1. the lion's	**a)** pace
2. at arm's	**b)** share
3. at a snail's	**c)** play
4. a bird's	**d)** length
5. child's	**e)** eye view
6. teacher's	**f)** pet

3. The sound /ər/ at the end of a word is often spelled **-or** as in **creator**, or **-er** as in <u>pitcher</u>. Rewrite each of the following occupations using the correct ending. Check your dictionary if necessary.

    a) doct_ _   **b)** lawy_ _

    c) teach_ _   **d)** investigat_ _

    e) wait_ _   **f)** profess_ _

    g) sculpt_ _   **h)** plumb_ _

4. Unscramble the following syllables to create four words from the Other Patterns list:

    a) va•e•tor•el

    b) es•nec•y•sar

    c) a•tor•cre

    d) quer•or•con

Some people confuse the order and number of the letters **c** and **s** in **necessary**. Just remember that the letter **c** comes before the letter **s** in the alphabet, and the number 1 (one **c**) comes before the number 2 (two **s's**) in counting.

1. **a)** Choose one of these survey topics (or a topic of your own) and write five questions that would require a *yes* or *no* answer. (Hint: You may wish to follow the model on page 87.)

   • friends you can trust • curfews • allowances • favourite pets

   b) Distribute at least twenty copies of your survey to friends, classmates, teachers, parents/guardians, and so on.

   c) Tally the results and share them with the class.

2. Rewrite the sentences from the passage below by using the possessive form of the underlined words.

   a) I can't wait for the <u>concession stand at the theatre</u> to open.

   b) Besides watching movies, a <u>favourite pastime of a teenager</u> is eating popcorn.

   c) <u>The feature this week</u> is about giant turtles who attack sewer workers during their lunch break.

   d) According to <u>a description given by one witness</u>, the turtles steal <u>a sandwich from a victim</u> and shove it into <u>the fuel tank of their submarine</u>.

   e) <u>The safety of society</u> hangs in the balance.

   f) But thanks to <u>the efforts of a retired umpire</u>, the turtles are invited to an all-you-can-eat buffet to re-fuel.

3. Here are items that relate to some of the list words. Write the list word that might appear before each item. Remember to write each word in the possessive form.

   a) whistle   **b)** big top   **c)** testimony

   d) periscope   **e)** shell   **f)** special effects

Verbs: Past Participles The past participle is used to express an action that starts in the past and continues into the present. The past participle is generally formed by combining the past tense of the verb with an auxiliary verb, such as *has, have,* or *had.* In the example, "The class <u>has competed</u> in the tournament every year," <u>has</u> is the present tense of *to have,* and <u>competed</u> is the past tense of *to compete.*

Present Participle	**verb + ing**	am/is/are + present participle = an action that takes place now	I <u>am walking</u> around the block. She <u>is walking</u> around the block. They <u>are walking</u> around the block.
Past Participle	**verb + ed** (also the past tense)	has/have/had + past participle = an action that starts in the past and continues into the present	I <u>have walked</u> around the block. He <u>has walked</u> around the block. They <u>had walked</u> around the block.

1. Use either the past-tense or past-participle form of the verb in parentheses to correctly complete these sentences.

a) Each time I _____ past the arena, I _____ and _____ to convince myself to enter the building. (to walk), (to stop), (to try)

b) Finally, I _____ up my courage and went inside. (to summon)

c) Most of the players _____ waiting for the game to start. (to be)

d) I _____ someone who _____ like the coach. (to approach), (to look)

e) I said that I had _____ to play on the team since the beginning of the year. (to want)

f) Everyone _____ to clap. They had _____ one more player all week! (to start), (to need)

2. Choose a piece of your writing and identify all the basic verb tenses you find (see The Editing Desk in Units 14–17 for some examples). Are there any verb tenses that you rarely use? Are there any verbs that look different from the ones you have studied so far? Make a chart of the verbs you use.

For Better or For Worse®   by Lynn Johnston

22 Possessives: Plural

chart allows you to display information a variety of ways. This chart shows how ural and possessive nouns are formed. By mparing these examples, we can see mmon patterns among the words.

Singular	Singular Possessive	Plural	Plural Possessive
student	student's	students	students'
turkey	turkey's	turkeys	turkeys'
butterfly	butterfly's	butterflies	butterflies'
watch	watch's	watches	watches'
woman	woman's	women	women's

Thinking about Words

butterflies'
children's
cookies'
enemies'
judges'
lockers'
parents'
passengers'
schools'
scientists'
students'
turkeys'
twins'
watches'
women's

OTHER PATTERNS
client
consumer
customer
*neighbour
*visible

1. Look at the first two columns of the chart above. Write a sentence that states the general rule for making a singular noun possessive, as in "The butterfly's wings were very delicate."

2. The third column shows the plural form of each noun. Compare the words in the third and fourth columns. Write a sentence stating the general rule for making a plural noun possessive, as in "The students' votes were counted."

3. Can you explain why in most cases an **s** is not added after the apostrophe when forming a plural possessive? Try saying "The students's votes were counted." What did you notice?

4. Since irregular plurals, such as <u>women</u> and <u>children</u>, do not end in **s**, it is easy to pronounce the plural possessive. Write the plural possessive form of *women* and *children*.

Word Pattern

- An apostrophe (**'**) is added to the end of the plural form of most words to show possession (**butterflies'**).

- An apostrophe + s (**'s**) is added to the end of irregular plurals, such as <u>children</u>, to form the plural possessive (**children's**).

1. Rewrite each sentence, substituting the underlined phrases with a plural possessive.

> **a)** The <u>eyes of the twins</u> lit up when they heard the <u>decision of the judges</u>.
>
> **b)** The <u>poems of the children</u> were displayed during the <u>meeting of the parents</u>.
>
> **c)** The <u>journey of the butterflies</u> to Mexico was tracked using computers.

2. The word **visible** comes from the Latin verb form *videre* meaning "to see." The words in the box also share this word origin. Complete each of the following sentences with one of the words.

visibility	visual	visibly	vision	invisible

> **a)** The accident victim was _____ shaken by the ordeal.
>
> **b)** At the height of the snowstorm there was zero _____ for driving.
>
> **c)** The crack in the vase was so tiny it was almost _____ to the eye.
>
> **d)** The search plane was able to make _____ contact with the stranded sailor.
>
> **e)** My _____ was impaired by the bright sunlight.

Writing and Revising

1. Choose a list word that is a plural possessive. List as many items as you can that might be associated with the word, then sort the items into two or more categories. Display the words in chart form. (Hint: Notice how items related to **schools'** have been organized in the chart below.)

Schools'		
Objects	**People**	**Events**
bookcases	principal	opening announcements
chairs	students	sports day
desks	teachers	spring concert

2. a) Write a short paragraph about each of these graphs. You might explain the results or comment on an interesting fact.

Income = $53.65

Books & Magazines 11%
Savings 12%
Tapes & CDs 23%
Movies 31%
Food Snacks 23%

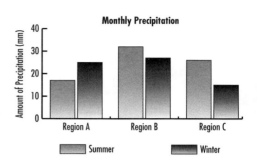

Monthly Precipitation

Amount of Precipitation (mm)

Region A   Region B   Region C

Summer   Winter

b) Why do you think this type of visual information often doesn't require an explanation?

The Editing Desk

Irregular Verbs: Past Tense Verbs that don't follow a regular pattern are called *irregular verbs*. Their past and past-participle tenses can't be formed by just adding **-ed**. Unfortunately, for someone trying to learn English grammar, these verbs can cause a lot of frustration. Here are some common examples of irregular verbs:

Infinitive	Past Tense	Past Participle
to begin	began	begun
to do	did	done
to fall	fell	fallen
to go	went	gone
to hurt	hurt	hurt
to lie	lay	lain

Can you spot the irregular, past-tense verbs in this paragraph from *Wild Dog Summer* by Jean Mills?

❝ Suddenly I felt exhausted. My head was swimming on my shoulders and it took all my strength to keep it straight. ❞

1. The underlined verb form in each of these sentences is incorrect. Rewrite the sentence using the correct verb form.

  a) The boat <u>sinked</u> after it struck a rock.

  b) They had <u>putted</u> the new dishes on the shelf.

  c) Who has <u>forgot</u> their tickets?

  d) Nobody <u>seen</u> her go inside the building.

  e) Chandra <u>tored</u> open her present.

  f) When they <u>heared</u> the siren, they <u>fleed</u> down the street.

2. Even irregular verbs have patterns. See how many verb tenses you can add for each of these irregular patterns. The first two have been done for you.

Present	Past	Past Participle
spin	*spun*	*spun*
break	*broke*	*broken*
drink		
sing		
swim		
bring		
buy		
think		

LANGUAGE MATTERS

Some past and past-participle verb endings are spelled two ways: **-ed** and **-t**. Both are acceptable, although the **-t** form is considered somewhat outdated. The following are common examples:

spelled / spelt	dreamed / dreamt	learned / learnt
burned / burnt	leaped / leapt	spilled / spilt

23 Related Words

Sssssss, searcher soon stumbles on snake's secret sanctuary

Headlines are designed to "hook" the reader so that she or he will read on. Do you wish you could read the articles accompanying these newspaper headlines? Your interest may have been sparked by the use of puns (cowed), sound devices (Who-o-o-o; Sssssss), or homophones (Bearly).

Bearly room to move at clinic:
Tots, toddlers seek first aid for teddy bears

Searchers cowed by missing angus steer

Who-o-o-o gives a hoot? Reclusive feathered friend draws fans

commerce
commercial
competition
dutiful
duty
image
imagine
maintain
maintenance
major
majority
political
politics
revise
revision

OTHER PATTERNS
*business
*column
foreign
rhyme
wrestle

Thinking about Words

1. The headlines above all deal with animals. Try to create a catchy headline about a different animal. Consider using puns, sound devices, or other plays on words.

2. When **-ive** is added to the end of a verb or a noun, the related word becomes an adjective. What is the base form of <u>reclusive</u>? What does it mean to be reclusive? Check your dictionary if you are unsure.

3. How many words can you list that are related to the base word <u>friend</u>? When you can't think of any more, look in a dictionary for additional words.

Word Pattern

Related words share a common base word and are usually related in spelling and meaning.

1. If you try to sound out the word **competition**, you will find the schwa vowel **e** difficult to hear. By remembering that the base word is compete, however, you will know that the schwa is spelled with an **e**.

Write the base word for each of the following. Notice that the underlined schwa vowel is clearly pronounced in the base word.

    a) combination

    b) opposition

    c) definition

    d) contribution

2. How many words can you write that are related to the base word **image**? In each example, underline the base word. Notice whether you have added prefixes or suffixes to the base.

3. a) When the suffix **-ful** is added to the word **duty**, the new word is **dutiful**. Follow this pattern by adding the same suffix to beauty and plenty.

    b) If people show mercy they are merciful. Does it then follow that people who show pity are pitiful? Consult a dictionary if you are unsure.

4. A number of the list words contain silent letters. Rewrite each of the following words, filling in the blanks with the correct letters. Then, highlight the letters.

    a) forei_n   **b)** colum_   **c)** bus_ness

    d) _restle   **e)** r_yme

5. The sound /r/ in **wrestle** is spelled **wr**. Many words in English begin with this spelling for the /r/ sound.

Complete the following puzzle with words that fit the meaning and spelling clues. A thesaurus may help you solve some of them.

    a) wr_ _ _ = to damage or destroy

    b) wr_ _ _ = great anger; rage

    c) wr_ _ _ _ _ = twist and turn; squirm

    d) wr_ _ _ _ = a ring of flowers or leaves

1. Find an interesting photo or illustration and write a headline for it that would capture a reader's attention.

2. Choose one of the headlines from page 95. Write the first paragraph of a newspaper article that might appear underneath the headline.

3. Use each pair of related list words in a sentence. For example, "I **imagine** the **image** is a fake."

4. Sometimes, words seem to be related because they often appear together. Do you know the meaning of these word-pair expressions?

    a) pride and joy   **b)** fast and furious

    c) rise and shine   **d)** cloak and dagger

LANGUAGE MATTERS

Words or expressions that are used to soften an unpleasant idea are called *euphemisms*. Although euphemisms are frequently used in spoken language, they can make your writing unclear. Here are some popular euphemisms:

- previously owned = used
- pass away = die
- downsized = fired
- genuine imitation = fake
- waste removal technician = garbage collector
- competitive salary = minimum wage

The Editing Desk

Subject–Verb Agreement The subject of a sentence must match or agree with its verb. This is especially true for the present tense (see chart below). Notice that an **s** is added to the verb in the third-person singular.

Subject–Verb Agreement		
Person	**Singular**	**Plural**
First Person	I taste.	We taste.
Second Person	You taste.	You taste.
Third Person	He / She / It tastes.	They taste.

1. Rewrite the following sentences using the correct present-tense form of the word in parentheses.

   a) The players _____ something new every day. (experience)

   b) A locked gate _____ anyone from entering. (prevent)

   c) Masa _____ too often to be a friend! (interfere)

   d) On Thursdays, Oodles of Noodles _____ applicants for the position. (interview)

2. The present tenses of **to be** and **to have** don't follow the subject–verb agreement pattern shown in the last activity. These two verbs are used to make many different tenses. Use the present tense of these verbs to complete the sentences that follow the chart.

Subject–Verb Agreement				
Present Tense	**Number**	**First Person**	**Second Person**	**Third Person**
to be	singular	I am.	You are.	He/She/It is.
	plural	We are.	You are.	They are.
to have	singular	I have.	You have.	He/She/It has.
	plural	We have.	You have.	They have.

   a) The children _____ skating on the pond. (to be)

   b) I'm afraid she _____ taken it with her. (to have)

   c) Only one person _____ allowed to wait in here. (to be)

   d) I _____ leaving in just a minute. (to be)

   e) Where _____ they gone? (to have)

3. Sometimes it is not easy to spot the subject of a sentence, especially when it is not positioned next to the verb. Complete these sentences with the correct form of the verb in parentheses. (Hint: In some sentences, you can choose either the present or the past tense.)

   a) The dog with all the fleas _____ waiting for a bath. (to be)

   b) Only members of this class _____ come to the dance. (to have)

   c) Too many people who do not have passes _____ allowed backstage. (to be)

   d) A bag of potato chips _____ not a complete meal! (to be)

   e) Only one of the top-selling CDs on the shelf _____ been sold at half price. (to have)

Working with Words

1. Each of the following words contains a letter that is silent or not clearly pronounced. Rewrite each word, highlighting the "tricky" letter in some way. You might underline it, write it in a different colour, or capitalize it.

environment	government	column
foreign	wrestle	rhyme

2. Make these passages more informal by substituting contractions for the underlined words:

a) <u>Does he not</u> know that <u>it is</u> too far to walk? The <u>theatre is</u> on the other side of town. If <u>we are</u> planning to get there before the movie starts, <u>we will not</u> make it if we walk.

b) If there <u>had not</u> been an automatic bank machine outside the theatre, we <u>could not</u> have afforded the price of admission. We <u>did not</u> know that the theatre <u>would not</u> accept our special passes for that movie.

3. The sound /ər/ at the end of words can be created by a number of different letter combinations, including **er**, **or**, and **re**. Complete each of these /ər/ words with the correct spelling:

a) conquer_ _   **b)** custom_ _   **c)** theat_ _

d) elevat_ _   **e)** consum_ _   **f)** creat_ _

4. Rewrite each of the following phrases in the possessive form using an apostrophe where appropriate.

a) the contents of the sandwich = the _____ contents

b) the problems of society = _____ problems

c) the favourite saying of your teacher = your _____ favourite saying

d) the complaints of the passengers = the _____ complaints

e) the findings of the scientists = the _____ findings

f) the opinions of the women = the _____ opinions

5. Combine the prefixes, suffixes, and base or root words in the chart below to form as many words as possible. In some cases, spelling changes will occur in the base word. You may combine two or more parts to form a word. For example:

• confide + ence = confidence
• pre + view + er = previewer
• naut + ic + al = nautical

Prefixes	Base or Root Words	Suffixes
pre	view	tion; sion
inter	naut	al
sub	fere	ly
auto	marine	er; or; ar
astro	vent	ic
in	mobile	ance; ence

Proofreading

Correct the spelling mistakes in this paragraph:

Were working on a media project that teaches us a lot about the bisness world. We have to create a product thats friendly to the enviroment and that custumers would want to buy. My group decided to write a book of excuses teenager's can use to answer parents' questions about why they havent cleaned there rooms, done their homework, taken out the garbage, etc. We've videotaped a comercial that were showing in the cafateria at lunch. At a price of only $2.00 a book, we think we'll be succesfull in selling a copy to the majorety of the kids in the school.

Dictionary Skills

Multiple Meanings One feature of English is that a single word can often have many meanings. The word <u>fine</u>, for example, has fourteen definitions as an adjective (among them fine hair; a fine time; fine linen; feeling fine), six as a noun, and two as an adverb. According to *Mother Tongue* by Bill Bryson, the word <u>fine</u> fills two full pages of one comprehensive dictionary and requires up to 5000 words of description.

Read the dictionary entry on page 101 for the word *column*.

col•umn (kol′əm)   **1** a slender, upright structure; pillar.   **2** anything that seems slender and upright like a column.   **3** in the armed forces, an arrangement of persons in rows one behind another.   **4** a line of ships or aircraft one behind another.   **5** a narrow division of a page reading from top to bottom, kept separate by a line or a blank space.   **6** a part of a newspaper used for a special subject or written by a special writer.   *n.*

There is often an illustrative sentence, printed in italic type, following the definition of an entry word. Read these illustrative sentences for *column* and match them with the number of the entry definition.

a) *A newspaper often has eight columns on a page.*

b) *Columns are usually made of stone, wood, or metal.*

c) *A column of smoke rose from the chimney.*

d) *I enjoy reading the children's column in the Saturday paper.*

Language Power

Metaphors Writers use metaphors to make their writing more expressive. Metaphors are figures of speech that link two seemingly different objects or ideas and point out a similarity between the two. The expression "heart of stone" is an example of a metaphor.

1. Some metaphors refer to parts of the body. Write the expression represented by each puzzle below:

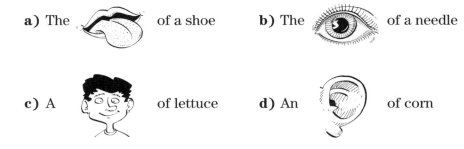

a) The [tongue image] of a shoe   **b)** The [eye image] of a needle

c) A [head image] of lettuce   **d)** An [ear image] of corn

Writers often create metaphors through the verbs they use. These verbs suggest actions or characteristics of the nouns on which they are based. For example, if someone is *monkeying around*, she or he is acting playfully or mischievously as a monkey would. The person is, therefore, compared with a monkey through the verb that is used.

2. The verbs and verb phrases below are all based on names in the animal world. Use each example in a sentence to show its meaning.

a) to horse around   **b)** to crow about   **c)** to parrot

d) to hound   **e)** to clam up

1. Design an experiment that would prove water has three states: gas, liquid, and solid. Use the experiment sheet on page 81 as your model. Include some of these list words in your experiment:

prediction	environment
maintain	visible
schools'	necessary
there's	except
successful	escape

2. An apostrophe is used to show possession or to signal that one or more letters have been left out of a word. Rewrite the paragraph below, inserting apostrophes where needed.

> Last Saturday Im coming out of the bathroom at the Mall. (Thats the one by the theatres entrance, near the childrens playroom.) Im about to say, "Hi guys, lets go," when I suddenly look around. Wheres everybody?
>
> I look up and Im staring at this store: Time Warp. Its filled with unusual timepieces. All the watches hands seem to be pointing at me! Then Ahmed taps me on my jackets sleeve. I jump and turn around. Everyones smiling at me. For a second, I didnt know where I was. The Malls revenge, I guess. Maybe its trying to tell me something.

3. Write an imaginary interview based on what one of the following list words suggests to you: referee, exercise, victim's, customer, wrestle. You may want to use an interview format that looks like this:

Interviewer: So, tell me, Gillian, what made you become a referee?
Gillian: Well, I was always bossing people around so I guess I....

4. Choose one list word from Units 21 or 22 that shows possession. Brainstorm a list of items that might relate to the word. (Hint: Use library resources such as encyclopedias, dictionaries, and other reference books.) For example:

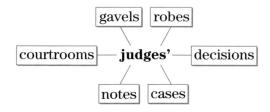

1. Write the correct form of the verb in parentheses to complete these sentences:

    a) They _____ not heard from him since last summer. (to have)

    b) We'_____ having trouble lifting this sofa bed. (to be)

    c) That magazine's cover _____ entirely new in design. (to be)

    d) Claire and Antonio have _____ on us for a ride all winter. (to rely)

    e) Please _____ the work finished by noon. (to have)

    f) Why _____n't she joined the drama and soccer clubs? (to have)

2. Write a sentence for each of the nouns below. What do all these nouns have in common?

    a) audience   **b)** team

    c) government   **d)** band (musical group)

3. Many of the verbs in the paragraph below have been used incorrectly. Rewrite the passage using the correct forms of the verbs.

> This is a true story. Last Saturday, I gone to the library to study. Usually I work in the back of the reading room, but this time I sit at the table by the front door. All of a sudden, I heared Gord and Teresa calling my name. When I lookt up, I must have hitted my notebook. The next thing I knowed, it was flying through the air like a missile. Gord, Teresa, and I watcht as it flied straight toward Jennifer, who was standing by the water cooler. She lookt up in time to see it coming, spinned around to avoid it, and accidentally hitted the water jug. It falled to the ground and sended a wave of water across the floor!

4. Which of the following nouns are singular and which are plural? Use each noun with a matching verb (singular or plural) in a sentence, or use them all in a paragraph. (Hint: These nouns are tricky. You may want to look them up in a dictionary.)

    a) comics   **b)** news

    c) pliers   **d)** mathematics

    e) pants   **f)** eyeglasses

    g) scissors   **h)** molasses

    i) statistics   **j)** United States

5. Complete each of these sentences using the present-participle or past-participle form of the verb in parentheses.

    a) Alan is _____ to learn how to play the violin. (to try)

    b) We have always _____ why those shows were so popular. (to wonder)

    c) The traffic is _____ for the lights to change. (to wait)

    d) Anyone who is _____ in the choir should sign the attendance sheet. (to sing)

    e) Lightning has _____ that building three times in the last year. (to strike)

Word Play

1. In crossword puzzles, you try to match the number of blank spaces to a clue. See if you can guess these crossword clues.

    a) This snake tightens a lot   ☐ o ☐

    b) An insect that sounds like a relative   ☐ ☐ t ☐

    c) An oil-rich country in the Middle East   K ☐ ☐ ☐ ☐ t ☐

    d) Round, fluffy clouds   ☐ u ☐ u ☐ u ☐

    e) A person who drives a boat or a plane   ☐ i ☐ o ☐

    f) A unit of measurement still used with automobile engines   ☐ ☐ r ☐ ☐ o ☐ ☐ r

2. If you re-arrange the letters of each word below, you can spell another word. How fast can you unscramble them?

    a) use   **b)** vase   **c)** ache

    d) sheet   **e)** unite   **f)** cause

3. Now here is a challenge. Unscramble the letters of these words to find two other words.

    a) paws   **b)** mate   **c)** dare

    d) diet   **e)** eats   **f)** inks

4. Each word below has a homophone that has something to do with food. Can you guess what it is?

    a) bury   **b)** serial   **c)** bred

    d) colonel   **e)** pair   **f)** weigh

LOST KITTEN

Disappeared near Roseland Plaza. **REWARD!**

IMPO$$IBLE PRICE$!
WHAT A DEAL!

UNBELIEVABLE MARKDOWNS!

NON-SMOKING AREA

disagree
disappointed
disobey
immature
impolite
impossible
irregular
irresistible
misunderstand
non-fiction
non-profit
uncomfortable
unconscious
unreasonable
unusual

OTHER PATTERNS
guidance
guilty
guitar
*league
*strength

A number of the words in these signs contain prefixes meaning "not." Can you find all six of them?

Thinking about Words

1. Long words are often easier to spell if we think of the base word first and then add prefixes and suffixes. Write an equation to show the structure of the word <u>disappeared</u>.

prefix + base + suffix = _____ + _____ + _____

2. Knowing how to relate the meaning of a prefix and base word will also help you to read longer words. For example, if you know that **ir-** means "not," then the word <u>irreplaceable</u> (ir + replace + able) means "cannot be replaced." Follow this example to write a definition for each of these words:

a) irresponsible **b)** misbehaviour

c) disapprove **d)** unappreciated

Word Pattern

Prefixes such as **dis-**, **im-**, **ir-**, **mis-**, **non-**, and **un-** are considered *prefixes of negation*; that is, they serve to negate the meaning of the base word.

Working with Words

1. Rewrite this dialogue and complete the blanks with words from the unit list.

> **Adult:** I was very dis_____ with your im_____ behaviour this evening. Was it un_____ of me to expect you to say hello to our guests? And don't you know it is im_____ to eat handfuls of appetizers without offering any to those around you?
>
> **Teenager:** I'm sorry, but the jumbo shrimp were im_____ to pass up. And the mini bagels were ir_____! I'll try to talk with your guests the next time you have a party. It's just that I feel un_____ when I meet so many strangers at once.

2. a) Combine the prefixes, base words, and suffixes to form five words. In some cases, the spelling of the base will change slightly when the suffix is added. Check the spelling in a dictionary if you are unsure.

Prefixes	Base Words	Suffixes
dis-	respect	-action
im-	perfect	-able
un-	happy	-ful
non-	tax	-tion
mis-	interpret	-ness

b) Write sentences using the five words you formed in part (a). Try to use as many of the words as you can in one sentence.

3. Three list words begin with the letter combination **gui** (**guidance**, **guilty**, **guitar**). The following words also follow this pattern but may be new vocabulary for you. Match the word with its meaning. Use a dictionary if you need help.

1. guise	**a)** sly tricks; crafty deceit
2. guinea	**b)** a society for mutual aid or for some common purpose
3. guile	**c)** a small flag or streamer carried as a guide by soldiers
4. guild	**d)** an amount equal to twenty-one shillings
5. guidon	**e)** a style of dress; garb

Notice this pattern:
strong — strength
long — length

4. Rebus puzzles use pictures, letters, or symbols to represent the sound of words or phrases. Can you solve the following puzzles?

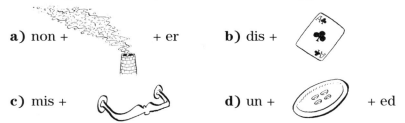

a) non +   + er   **b)** dis +

c) mis +   **d)** un +   + ed

Writing and Revising

1. Rewrite this sign substituting some of the words with list words that mean the opposite. (Hint: If necessary, change or delete some words.)

2. Choose a "not" list word. Write a paragraph that uses the meaning of the word as a focus. For example, something you have been **disappointed** about; an **impossible** task you have completed; why people **misunderstand** you.

3. Make up a display sign for one of the following situations. Try using some list words in your sign.

    a) The Telephone Warehouse's "Talk-Till-You-Drop" sale

    b) *Nevermore* — a new underarm deodorant

    c) The Locks Nest — Monster sale

    d) The Lively Wrecking Company's open house

    e) The Hot Spot Travel Agency's seat sale of the century

The Editing Desk

Easily Confused Verbs Some verbs are challenging to learn because they look similar to other verbs. Here are three common examples:

- **lay/lie:** *to lay* means "to place something down"; *to lie* means "to assume or be in a horizontal or flat position"
- **sit/set:** *to sit* means "to rest on the lower part of the body; to be in a state of rest"; *to set* means "to put or place something in a location"
- **rise/raise:** *to rise* means "to get up from a lying, sitting, or kneeling position"; *to raise* means "to lift up or cause to rise"

For some of these verbs, the past participles are not regular: they don't end in **-ed**. The chart below shows their differences.

Verb	Present	Past	Past Participle
to lay	lay(s)	laid	laid
to lie	lie(s)	lay	lain
to sit	sit(s)	sat	sat
to set	set(s)	set	set
to rise	rise(s)	rose	risen
to raise	raise(s)	raised	raised

1. Which sentence in each of these pairs is correct?

   a) After the thunderstorm, the moon raised high above the clouds.
   After the thunderstorm, the moon rose high above the clouds.

   b) "Why don't you set awhile," she said to me.
   "Why don't you sit awhile," she said to me.

   c) The dog lay on the pavement without moving.
   The dog laid on the pavement without moving.

   d) I was told that they have always laid the dishes on the table like th
   I was told that they have always lain the dishes on the table like th

2. Choose the correct verb and tense for each sentence.

   a) We all waited with Marina while she _____ in the dentist's chair. (to sit, to set)

   b) "I don't understand why you have to _____ around the house all day!" (to lay, to lie)

   c) This bread dough _____ in one hour. (to rise, to raise)

   d) David watched anxiously as she _____ her cards on the table. (to lay, to lie)

26 Suffixes

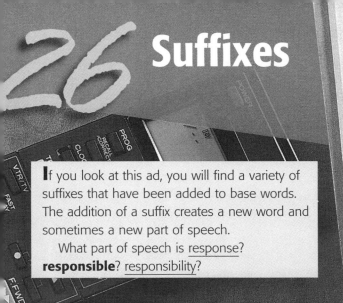

If you look at this ad, you will find a variety of suffixes that have been added to base words. The addition of a suffix creates a new word and sometimes a new part of speech.

What part of speech is <u>response</u>? **responsible**? <u>responsibility</u>?

Coming Attractions!

Action-packed thrillers
★
Romantic comedies
★
Home improvement tips
★
Musicals
★
Responsible news coverage
★

You'll find it all on PXYN-TV!

28

attention
attraction
available
conclusion
confusion
conversation
decision
description
edible
education
horrible
lovable
responsible
separation
valuable

OTHER PATTERNS

cruise
juicy
nuisance
*weird
*worst

Thinking about Words

1. Complete these word equations in your notebook as follows:
   response + ible = responsible

   a) _____ + _____ = improvement
   b) _____ + _____ = musical
   c) _____ + _____ = action
   d) _____ + _____ = romantic

2. Examine the word equations you wrote in the activity above.

   a) Which equation involves changing the last consonant in the base word to a different consonant before adding the suffix?

   b) Which equation drops a letter **t** from the base before the suffix is added?

   c) Which two equations require no spelling change to the base word before the suffix is added?

Word Pattern

When a suffix is added to a base word, the part of speech often changes. The new word may also require a spelling change to the base word.

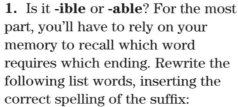

SPELLING SECRETS

Generally, if a suffix begins with a vowel, the final **e** is dropped from the base (move + able = movable). If the suffix begins with a consonant, the final **e** often stays with the base word (move + ment = movement).

1. Is it **-ible** or **-able**? For the most part, you'll have to rely on your memory to recall which word requires which ending. Rewrite the following list words, inserting the correct spelling of the suffix:

a) respons_ble   **b)** avail_ble   **c)** valu_ble

d) horr_ble   **e)** ed_ble   **f)** lov_ble

2. a) Compare these base words with their derived forms. What happens to each base word when the suffix is added? Does the suffix begin with a vowel or a consonant?

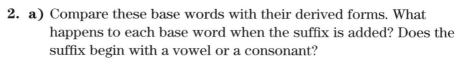

converse ⟶ conversation   love ⟶ lovable

response ⟶ responsible   value ⟶ valuable

b) Complete these word equations in your notebook. Remember the pattern you observed in part (a).

mature + ation = _____   sense + ible = _____

desire + able = _____   invite + ation = _____

3. "Try our juicy, charbroiled burgers!" Can't you just taste these delicious burgers? Words such as **juicy** are very descriptive. Like all onomatopoeic words, the sound of the word almost imitates the sound of the thing being described.

Suggest some words to describe the following products. Try to choose descriptive words that appeal strongly to the senses.

a) taco mix   **b)** hand soap   **c)** brand of orange juice

4. The following pairs of words all contain the vowel combination **ui**. Only one word in each pair, however, uses **ui** to create the sound /oo/ as in stew. Write down the word from each pair that contains the /oo/ sound. The circled letters in the correct words will spell the answer to this riddle: What do you call a mangled dog after a run-in with a tough cat?

a) circ(u)it / (c)ruiser   **b)** s(l)uice / squ(i)d

c) suit(a)ble / se(q)uin   **d)** pengu(i)n / purs(u)it

e) (b)uild / bruise(d)   **f)** r(e)cruit / requi(r)e

Answer: **a)** __ **b)** __ **c)** __ **d)** __ **e)** __ **f)** __

1. **a)** Choose a type of television program from the ad on page 109. Think of a title for a new show. Write a paragraph advertising the show using these words: **attraction**, **horrible**, **lovable**, **valuable**, **weird**.

   b) Apart from the list words, how many other words ending in suffixes did you use in your paragraph? Add these words to your personal word list.

2. Each of these list words has more than one dictionary meaning. Write a sentence for each meaning.

   a) attraction   **b)** separation   **c)** responsible   **d)** available

3. Rewrite the sentences below, correcting the misspelled list words.

   a) The discription the police got didn't match the person in custody.

   b) First of all, this suspect seemed very lovible.

   c) Secondly, his background didn't suggest such a horrable crime.

   d) The wurst thing he had done was make a newsance of himself in a fast-food restaurant.

   e) He tried to get the cashier's attension by sticking out his tongue.

   f) That may not have been a responsable act, but it wasn't a crime!

   g) Since the suspect provided no valueable leads in the case, the dicision was made to release him.

LANGUAGE MATTERS

The root of the word **description** is *scribe*, meaning "a person who writes" or "the action of marking something." Notice that the **b** changes to a **p** when the suffix **-tion** is added. In what way do the letters change in these related word pairs?

| absorb ⋯⟶ absorption | conceive ⋯⟶ conception |
| satisfy ⋯⟶ satisfaction | sign ⋯⟶ signature |

The Editing Desk

Quotations A quotation is the actual words a person uses. There are two types of quotations, as follows:

Direct quotation: the exact words of a speaker
Indirect quotation: the approximate words a speaker uses

Direct Quotation	Indirect Quotation
• Example: "The movie was very enjoyable," she said. • enclosed in double quotation marks (" ") • comma separates the quotation from the speaker • first word is often capitalized • punctuation is positioned inside the quotation marks	• Example: He said that he was glad to be here. • does not require quotation marks • conjunction *that* is often used in front of the speaker's words • first word is never capitalized

Notice the way quotations have been used in this excerpt from *Blueberries and Whipped Cream* by Sylvia McNicoll.

66 I turned away and walked straight into Mark. "Oh, sorry," I said and bent down to help him pick up his books.

He was trying to pick them up by himself and we accidentally bumped heads.

"Ouch," he said.

"Sorry again," I handed him his books.

"It's O.K.," he said sadly as though he were pardoning me for killing his pet cat. 99

1. Insert the correct punctuation marks in the following sentences.

   a) I always thought I'd like to be a firefighter she told us.

   b) Becoming a nurse was out she admitted. I hate the sight of blood.

   c) A lead singer in a group sounded like a great career she explained but I was tone deaf.

   d) She stated that she also thought about becoming a scientist.

   e) Nothing I decided to become interested me for long she told us.

   f) Then with a gleam in her eye she added until I discovered flying.

2. **a)** Write about one of the following situations. Include dialogue and be sure to add quotation marks where necessary.
   * baby-sitting a younger child
   * ordering from a rude waiter or waitress
   * meeting a friend while waiting for a bus
   * a situation of your choice

   b) Rewrite your passage and include some indirect quotations.

Specialized Words: Careers

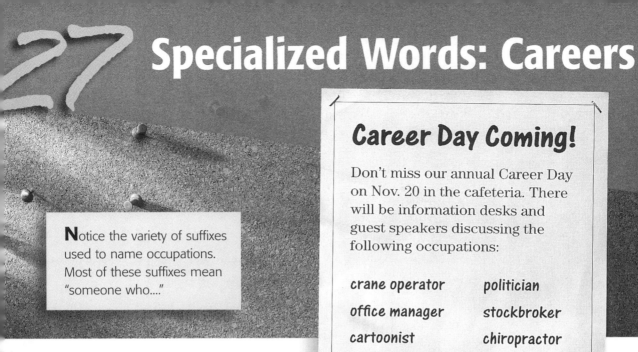

Career Day Coming!

Don't miss our annual Career Day on Nov. 20 in the cafeteria. There will be information desks and guest speakers discussing the following occupations:

crane operator	politician
office manager	stockbroker
cartoonist	chiropractor
restaurateur	musician
psychologist	

Notice the variety of suffixes used to name occupations. Most of these suffixes mean "someone who...."

architect
author
biologist
dentist
electrician
engineer
firefighter
lawyer
machinist
mechanic
nurse
programmer
scientist
technician
valet

OTHER PATTERNS
belief
*ceiling
grief
*receive
yield

Thinking about Words

1. The /ər/ sound at the end of a word can be spelled in a number of ways, including **-or** or **-er**. You just have to remember which spelling fits a given word. Organize the occupations listed in the Career Day ad in two columns according to the spelling of the /ər/ sound.

2. The suffix **-cian** in <u>musician</u> and <u>politician</u> sounds like /shən/. Can you think of at least two other ways of spelling a suffix to create this sound? Find a word example for each suffix.

3. Many career-related words are formed by adding **-ist** to a base word. What two words from the advertisement end in **-ist**? Write a definition for each using the formula, "A _____ is someone who _____."

Word Pattern

There are several common spelling patterns for the ending of words naming careers. These include **-ist** (**dentist**), **-or** and **-er** (<u>doctor</u>, <u>trainer</u>), and **-cian** (<u>magician</u>).

1. Rewrite the following list words and complete the blanks with either -er or -or.

    a) lawy_ _   **b)** programm_ _   **c)** auth_ _   **d)** firefight_ _

2. **a)** The following occupations all apply to careers in business. Complete each word with either **-er** or **-or**. Then, match each meaning with the correct occupation. A dictionary will help with both the spelling and the meaning.

Occupation	Meaning
1. treasur_ _ 4	**a)** a person who sells directly to consumers
2. direct_ _ 3	**b)** outsider brought in to settle a dispute
3. mediat_ _ 2	**c)** top corporate executive
4. supervis_ _ 5 6	**d)** chief financial officer of a company
5. retail_ _ 1	**e)** superintendent or manager of a unit in a busin

  b) Answer this riddle using the code numbers appearing under the letters in the first column of part (a):

    Q: What do you call a parrot that joins the military?

    A: __ __ __ __ __ __ __ __ __ __ __ __ __ __ !
       2   5 2 1 1 6 3   3 1 6 6 5 4 1

3. Language that represents both males and females is called "inclusive language." In the past, titles given to many occupations have excluded one gender. For example, the term *fireman* makes it seem as though only men can fight fires. The more "inclusive" title that is currently used is **firefighter**. Do you know the non-sexist version of these words?

    a) salesman   **b)** mailman

    c) workman   **d)** chairman

    e) policeman   **f)** mankind

NOUN OVERBOARD!

©1995 Tribune Media Services, Inc. All Rights Reserved. 2-21

Charlie tries not to be sexist.

Reprinted with permission—Toronto Star Syndicate.

4. a) The rule "**i** before **e** except after **c**" applies to the Other Patterns words. Sort them as follows:

i before **e**: _____ _____ _____

except after **c**: _____ _____

b) Using the rule above, complete these words with either **ie** or **ei**.

f_ _rce   dec_ _ve   p_ _ce   n_ _ce

Writing and Revising

1. a) Choose a career-related list word and, with a partner, brainstorm a list of words and phrases that are associated with that career.

b) Use as many of the words from part (a) as you can in a paragraph describing the career.

2. a) Which careers in the unit list end in something other than **-or**, **-er**, or **-ist**?

b) Here are some descriptions of other occupations that do not contain the suffix patterns described above. Do you know them?

- a person who cares for the health of animals
- a female ballet dancer
- a restaurant cook
- a person who looks after passengers on airplanes
- a salesperson in a store
- a person who makes people laugh

The Editing Desk

Pronoun Problems Pronouns can add variety and interest to your writing. If pronouns are used incorrectly, however, they can alter the meaning of your message and confuse your reader.

- **I** and **me**

  I is a subject pronoun. It can begin a sentence. **Me** is called an object pronoun because it comes after a preposition or a verb.

  > This gift is for you and I. (incorrect)
  > This gift is for you and me. (correct)

- **he/she** and **him/her**

  He and **she** are subject pronouns. **Him** and **her** are object pronouns.

  > Him and her had to take the bus. (incorrect)
  > He and she had to take the bus. (correct)

1. Choose either **I** or **me** to correctly complete the following sentences:
   a) The traffic light turned green just as Darshan and _____ jumped on the bus.
   b) The driver turned to _____ and asked if _____ had paid my fare.
   c) Of course _____ had paid my fare, but she hadn't seen _____ do it.
   d) Darshan and _____ tried to explain, but the driver ordered _____ off the bus.
   e) Finally, a woman came forward to tell the driver that _____ had paid the fare.
   f) The bus driver apologized for doubting _____.
   g) We were both glad (Darshan and _____) since neither he nor _____ had any more money.

2. Use one of the choices given in parentheses to complete these sentences:
   a) I was talking to Wanda when _____ walked in. (he, him)
   b) We looked at _____ as _____ sat down at a table next to us. (he, him), (he, him)
   c) Then Wanda looked away but I could tell _____ wanted to talk to _____. (she, her), (he, him)
   d) I couldn't stand to see _____ suffer. (she, her)
   e) Over Wanda's silent objection, I dragged _____ over to meet _____. (she, her), (he, him)
   f) We sat down beside _____ and I introduced Wanda. (he, him)
   g) I could see that _____ and _____ were going to get along just fine! (she, her), (he, him)

LANGUAGE MATTERS

Using **who** and **whom** correctly should be simple, but it isn't.
• **Who** is a subject pronoun. It goes with a verb to complete a sentence. Example: "Who wants to go shopping?"
• **Whom** is an object pronoun. It follows either a preposition or a verb. Example: "With whom are you going?" (follows the preposition *with*). "Everyone knows whom Coach Yashinski will choose for Captain" (follows the verb *knows*).

Unfortunately, when the preposition is omitted, it makes it difficult to decide which pronoun (*who* or *whom*) should be used. Because *who* is often used incorrectly in place of *whom*, some experts predict that *whom* will eventually disappear from our language.

Words From Other Languages

Bizarre Accident at Charity Bazaar

Have you ever wondered where words in English come from? The words in these headlines are borrowed from at least five other languages. Can you guess what those languages are? Read on!

Gourmet Chefs Create Canapés

Influenza Outbreak: Patients Quarantined

Thinking about Words

alcohol
ballot
barbecue
cafeteria
career
carrot
coupon
garage
geography
physician
pioneer
prairie
restaurant
syrup
yacht

OTHER PATTERNS
*banquet
*because
occasion
raccoon
warranty

1. Homophones challenge even the best spellers in English. Notice the words <u>bizarre</u> and <u>bazaar</u> in the first headline. These words may sound alike, but they follow the spelling patterns of their language of origin. *Bizarre* comes from French, *bazaar* is taken from Persian. One of the homophones means "a place for the sale of many kinds of goods," and the other means "odd; fantastic." Do you know which meaning goes with which word?

2. Three of the four words in the second headline come from the French language. Rewrite these words, then look up their meaning(s) in the dictionary.

3. Both the words <u>influenza</u> and <u>quarantined</u> come from Italian. "Quarantine" is derived from the Italian word *quarantina*, which itself was borrowed from Latin *quadraginta*, meaning "forty." Persons, animals, plants, and so forth were put in isolation for forty days if there was suspicion that a cargo ship might be carrying a disease. List other words that you know have been borrowed from other languages.

Word Pattern

Many English words have been borrowed from other languages. This can result in spelling challenges because the borrowed words may use spelling patterns from the language of origin.

*equently misspelled word

1. The combining form **-graph** means "to make a picture, draw, or write," and comes from the Greek *graphein*, meaning "to write." This combining form may also refer to a machine that makes a picture, draws, or writes.

   a) Write at least five words that contain **-graph**. In each case, briefly explain how the word relates to the definition of graph.

   b) The word **geography** is composed of *geo*, meaning "land or earth," and *graph*. A word equation would be geo + graph + y.

   Write a definition of the word based on the parts given.

2. The following list words contain either double vowels or consonants. Rewrite the words in your notebook using the correct double letters.

   a) o_ _asion   **b)** pion_ _r   **c)** ca_ _ot

   d) wa_ _anty   **e)** ra_ _ _ _n   **f)** ba_ _ot

   g) car_ _r

3. Unscramble the following sets of syllables to form list words:

   a) ra•og•phy•ge   **b)** co•al•hol

   c) te•caf•a•ri•e   **d)** tau•res•rant

4. Many words related to food are borrowed from other languages. For example, **restaurant**, **banquet**, and **carrot** come from French, **barbecue** and **cafeteria** from Spanish, and **alcohol** and **syrup** from Arabic.

   a) Sort the following list of words into these six categories: Meat/Fish, Vegetables, Desserts, Beverages, Spices. You may need to consult a dictionary if you don't recognize some of these items.

   cappuccino (Italian)   broccoli (Italian)
   meringue (French)   sauerkraut (German)
   yogurt (Turkish)   paprika (Hungarian)
   chocolate (Spanish)   ginger (Sanskrit)
   pastrami (Yiddish)

   b) Plan a menu (a French word) using the items in part (a). Try to include a variety of language backgrounds in your selections.

1. Many English words, such as the following, come from the French language. Use each word in a sentence to show its meaning.

a) traitor	**b)** petty	**c)** sovereign
d) fatigue	**e)** poultry	**f)** felony

CALVIN AND HOBBES © 1992 Watterson. Reprinted with permission of UNIVERSAL PRESS SYNDICATE. All rights reserved.

2. Choose five list words and make up a headline using each word. Write the opening line of a story that might go with each headline.

3. a) The word **barbecue** has an unusual abbreviation. Do you know what it is?

b) What do these abbreviations stand for?

• P.S.	• Mrs.	• PC	• C.A.D.
• Anon.	• EKG	• NHL	• TGIF

4. In addition to **raccoon**, how many other animal names can you think of that have a double consonant? List at least five of them.

The Editing Desk

Matching Pronouns to Nouns Pronouns have to match their subjects. Using the correct pronouns in a sentence that has many nouns can challenge even the best writers. Look at the following sample sentences:

Simone told Emma that she had no business interfering. (unclear)
Simone told Emma that Emma had no business interfering. (clear)
Simone told Emma that she (Simone) had no business interfering. (clear)

Who does the pronoun *he* refer to in the last line of this passage from Max Braithwaite's novel *The Muffled Man*?

66 Chris edged forwards and peered round the corner again, as the digging finally stopped. The muffled man was brushing the dirt from... the rubble. As Chris watched, he pried open the lid and lifted out the contents. 99

1. Rewrite the sentences below so that the pronouns match the correct nouns, or change the pronoun so that it matches the right noun or nouns.

a) She took the sweater out of the drawer and wrapped it up.

b) The ball slowly rolled into the net, but it was already over.

c) Susan didn't believe Luciana when she said she was never there.

d) Pry off the tire from the rim and check it for leaks.

e) The other clothes were highlighted by its bright green colour.

f) Each of the shoes made their mark on the floor.

2. In English, there are plural pronouns that stand for people, whether male or female (*they, them, their*). There is, however, no singular pronoun that includes both males and females. At one time, *he, him,* and *his* were used to represent individuals of either gender, but this practice is no longer acceptable. Change the pronouns in these sentences so that both males and females are represented.

a) No one has to stay in his seat after the bell.

b) A library user should take care of his books.

c) Every doctor should listen to his patients.

d) Each person should prepare himself for the test.

LANGUAGE MATTERS

Here is an explanation of how some common words worked their way from other languages into English:

- The word <u>echo</u> was the name of a Roman nymph (a minor female goddess) who always repeated the last words she heard.
- The word <u>panic</u> developed from the name of a Greek nature god, *pan*, who would dash out from behind bushes to frighten people.
- The word <u>utopia</u> was first coined in 1516 by English writer Sir Thomas More. It is the word for an imaginary perfect society and is based on three Greek roots: *ou* meaning "no," *topos* meaning "place," and *ia* meaning "state of being."

29 New Words

New words are being added to the English language all the time, many from the world of technology. Some are compound words, others are acronyms, still others are old words that have been given new meanings. Do you know the meaning of all the computer-related terms in this paragraph?

Thinking of Buying a Computer?

There are so many **things** to consider when selecting **an** expensive item. First of all, what **do you** want a computer for? Desktop publishing? Surfing the Net? Preparing homework assignments? Telecommuting? Playing multimedia CD-ROMs? Secondly, do you want a brand name **or** a clone, a desktop or a laptop? Thirdly, what type of hardware and software will you need to ensure your computer will do all you want it to do, **and** more? The options are seemingly endless.

Thinking about Words

arcade
cursor
download
fax
hardware
interface
laptop
lifestyle
microchip
modem
mouse
notebook
software
spell checker
spreadsheet
teleshopping

OTHER PATTERNS

*cousin
curious
*interrupt
mysterious
various

1. New words are being formed all the time. The word <u>multimedia</u> is formed from the prefix **multi-**, meaning "many," and the base word <u>media</u>. The word *multimedia* refers to software that incorporates a variety of media. Can you think of other computer terms that contain the prefix **multi-**?

2. Some new words take the form of acronyms. What acronym appears in the sample paragraph? What does it stand for?

3. Other new words involve shortening a longer version. The term <u>Internet</u> is a combination of the prefix **inter-**, meaning "between," and the base word <u>network</u>. The word <u>internetwork</u> is shortened or "clipped" to *internet* and then capitalized to show it is a proper noun, not just a general term. Popular use has shortened it further to *the Net.*

What does <u>e-mail</u> stand for? Why is regular mail sometimes referred to as *snail mail*?

4. New expressions have also been added to our language via the world of technology. When people use the Internet, they often say they are "surfing the Net." How does this expression describe Internet use?

Word Pattern

New words are being created in English all the time. These words are sometimes shortened forms of longer words, new compound words, or old words given new meanings.

1. Many newly formed words in English are actually compound words. Two existing words that have a logical connection in meaning are combined to form another word. Write a word equation for each of the following list words, then explain the connection between the base words. For example, lap + top = laptop, a computer small enough to rest on your lap.

    a) notebook

    b) spreadsheet

    c) spell checker

    d) download

2. The prefix **micro-**, meaning "very small," is often used to describe new inventions in technology. The list word **microchip**, for example, means "a very small computer chip."

    Write at least five words beginning with **micro-** and explain why this prefix fits the meaning of the term. A dictionary will help you.

3. Jargon is the specialized vocabulary of a group of people. Many fields, such as sports, politics, law, the military, medicine, and so on, boast a language all their own. The field of technology leads the way, however, with jargon being added almost daily.

    Try to explain these expressions to someone who has little or no background in computers:

    a) The hackers broke into the government files.

    b) Just drag the cursor by sliding the mouse slowly.

    c) My hard drive crashed and wiped out my project!

    d) After you log on to the server, check the bulletin board for any new messages.

4. Many adjectives end in **-ous** or **-ious**. Complete the puzzle below:

Base Words	Adjectives
a) vary	_ _ _ious
b) fury	_ _ _ious
c) glory	_ _ _ _ious
d) luxury	_ _ _ _ _ious
e) mystery	_ _ _ _ _ _ious
f) victory	_ _ _ _ _ _ious

1. Headline-news articles follow a specific format based on the five Ws: Who? What? When? Where? Why? Answers to these questions must appear within the first paragraph, and often within the first sentence! It's not easy. Try it for yourself. Write an opening paragraph for each of the following newspaper headlines.

    a) Dog rescues child from ice   **b)** Total eclipse a total failure

    c) New "super food" a scam   **d)** Playoff fever comes to town

2. How many words beginning with the prefix **multi-** or **inter-** can you recall? List your words in chart form. Here are two to get you started:

    multi + cultural = <u>multicultural</u>   inter + national = <u>international</u>

3. Here are some trivia questions based on the new words in this unit.

    a) What does a **laptop** and a **notebook** have in common?

    b) **Fax** is a short form for what word?

    c) What is the opposite of **software**?

    d) What is the opposite of **download**?

    e) What do **spreadsheet** programs and databases have in common?

    f) Which list word is an input device?

LANGUAGE MATTERS

Computer technology has created dozens of new words and abbreviations. Here are some common and not-so-common examples. How many can you explain?

cyberspace	H.T.M.L.	scanner
truetype	Pascal	DOS

The Editing Desk

Writing Sentences A simple sentence has one subject and one verb.

subject verb
Alan   ran.

subject   verb
Three cars   passed   the corner.

Some ideas, however, are too complicated to be written in a simple sentence. Page 124 lists some sentence constructions that can be used to communicate more complex ideas.

Compound Sentences: two sentences connected by a conjunction. Compound sentences allow you to connect similar or opposing ideas. A comma is used before the connecting word.

sentence 1   comma conjunction   sentence 2

The clocked ticked away   ,   and   the time was running out.

Compound Subject: two nouns connected by a conjunction that, together, act as the subject of a sentence. With compound subjects you don't have to write the same sentence over again.

Rebecca met us later. Chun met us later.

can be rewritten as

subject 1   conjunction   subject 2

Rebecca   and   Chun   met us later.

Compound Verb: combining verbs, just like combining nouns, also helps to get rid of unnecessary sentences.

The river overflowed. The river ran down the bank.

can be rewritten as

verb 1   conjunction   verb 2

The river   overflowed   and   ran   down the bank.

1. Rewrite the sentence pairs to form one compound sentence. Use one of these conjunctions:

- *and* if the sentences relate to each other
- *but* if the sentences have opposing points of view
- *because* if there is a cause-effect relationship between the sentences

    a) We played all day in the tournament. Everyone had a great time.

    b) The sun rose at five. It was still overcast at ten.

    c) First add a cup of milk. Then slowly beat in two eggs.

    d) My library books are not due until next month. I will bring them back on Saturday.

    e) We had to load the dishwasher. Every dish in the house was dirty.

2. Simplify each pair of sentences by creating one sentence.

    a) Samir likes historical novels. Tyler likes historical novels.

    b) The dog sat up. It looked at us.

    c) The car sputtered. The car then stopped.

    d) Toni quickly came down the stairs. She went out the front door.

    e) The picnic was fun. The picnic was relaxing.

Working with Words

1. Replace each underlined phrase with a word containing a prefix meaning "not." Rewrite the sentence making any other necessary changes. The first one has been done for you.

   a) I am <u>not sure</u> about the time. *I am unsure of the time.*

   b) Are you <u>not comfortable</u> in that position?

   c) This deadline is <u>not possible</u> to meet.

   d) You obviously <u>did not understand</u> the question.

   e) My favourite books are those that are <u>not fiction</u>.

   f) The pattern on this sweater is <u>not regular</u>.

2. Unscramble the following four- and five-syllable list words.

   a) re•i•ble•sist•ir   **b)** ol•gist•o•bi   **c)** og•phy•ra•ge

   d) lec•cian•e•tri   **e)** ri•ous•mys•te   **f)** te•caf•a•e•ri

3. The words in each set below share a common spelling pattern. Identify the pattern and add other words that could belong to the set. Example:

Word Set	Common Pattern	Other Words
mysterious / various / luxurious	**-ious** ending	curious / furious

   a) firefighter / lifestyle / hardware / notebook

   b) guidance / guess / guitar / league

   c) physician / musician / technician / politician

   d) author / sculptor / conductor / cursor

4. Complete the words below with one of these sets of double consonants: **ll, rr, cc**.

   a) ra_ _oon   **b)** ca_ _ot   **c)** o_ _asion

   d) inte_ _upt   **e)** ba_ _ot   **f)** wa_ _anty

SPELLING SECRETS

Prefixes meaning "not" include **mis-**, **ir-**, **un-**, **non-**, and **im-**.

5. The following list words fit the rule "**i** before **e** except after **c**."

belief   ceiling   grief   receive   yield

   a) Rewrite each word under one of the following two headings:
     <u>i</u> before <u>e</u> and <u>except after</u> **c**.

   b) Add as many other words as you can to each category.

6. Supply the letter to complete each of the words below. In each case, the missing letter is a schwa vowel that is difficult to hear when you say the word. Try to remember it visually.

   a) sci_ntist
   b) eng_neer
   c) arch_tect

   d) m_chinist
   e) alc_hol
   f) barb_cue

Proofreading

Rewrite the passage below and correct all the misspelled list words.

Today we had Carreer Day at school. There were lots of guest speakers. There was an arkitect, an auther, a biologist, an enginear, a fire fighter, a loyer, and even a conductor. We helped a chef peel carots, we listened to a nerse explain how dangerous alchohol can be, and we watched a programer write a message in a computer language! Becuse there were so many speakers to choose from, no one left disapointed.

Dictionary Skills

Etymology Dictionary entries often contain information about the etymology or origin of the word. In the Gage dictionary, a fistnote symbol ☞ is used to signal etymology. Abbreviations of some common languages are used, as shown below:

OE	Old English (before A.D. 1100)
ME	Middle English (about 1100–1450)
AN	Anglo-Norman (1066–about 1350)
OF	Old French (before 1400)
F	French (modern)
Cdn.F	Canadian French
ON	Old Norse (before 1300)
L	Latin (classical–about 200 B.C. to A.D. 300)
Med.L	Medieval Latin (about 700–1500)
Gk.	Greek (classical—about 900 B.C. to A.D. 200)

Here is the word history that appears in the dictionary for the word *syrup*:

> **Syrup** comes from OF *sirop* or Med. L *sirupus*, which came from colloquial Arabic *sharāb* 'a drink' from *shariba* 'to drink'.

1. Use the abbreviation code in the etymology chart on page 126 to translate the information listed for *syrup*.

2. The following words have interesting etymologies. Use a dictionary to find some information about their origins

a) alligator	**b)** crescent	**c)** dollar
d) electric	**e)** ghoul	**f)** hippopotamus

Language Power

Redundancies The English language is filled with expressions that are needlessly wordy or repetitive. These are known as *redundancies*. The phrase *at this point in time*, for example, simply means "now." The expressions *aches and pains, bought and paid for*, and *ranting and raving* repeat the meaning within the expressions themselves.

1. Replace each of the following phrases with a simpler version that has the same meaning:

a) plain and simple	**b)** the honest truth
c) past experience	**d)** complimentary free gift

2. Rewrite this paragraph, replacing redundant expressions with simpler language.

Never in your life will you believe what happened to me at the mall yesterday! I went into the drugstore to buy some shampoo—you know, the "new and improved" one they keep advertising. I had bought and paid for it and was leaving the store when a security guard stopped me and accused me of stealing a magazine. I had brought the exact same one into the store and he thought I had stolen it! I explained what had happened and he let me go free and clear. I was so totally embarrassed—I just wanted it to be over and done with! Anyway, I arrived home safe and sound. To tell you the honest truth, I don't think I'll ever in my life go into that store again.

1. Imagine that you are the owner of a retail store. Design a window display sign advertising a special sale (see the example that follows). Use at least five of these list words in your sign:

attention	conclusion	coupon	fax	irresistible
mysterious	occasion	receive	scientist	unusual

2. You will have to rely on the sounds of letters to find the list words that are represented by these puzzles.

    a) love a ball   **b)** <u>stand</u>   **c)** π   **d)** Al K. Hall
                                     Miss   ear

3. Choose one of the headlines below and write the opening paragraph of a newspaper story that might follow the headline.

    a) Cafeterias Riot—Not Enough Spinach!

    b) Mysterious Spell Checker <u>Mispells</u> Words

    c) "I'm Not Guilty," Dentist Claims

    d) Weird Light Closes Highway

4. Here are the first lines of four stories. Complete a paragraph for one of them. Be sure to include a title for your paragraph.

    a) The disappointed crowd refused to leave after the game was over.

    b) "I don't care if you are a firefighter," he yelled. "There is *no* fire!"

    c) Carefully, the microchip was inserted into the slice of pizza.

    d) For twelve days the yacht floated without direction, its engine and generator silent.

1. Simplify the sentences below by using compound sentences, subjects, or verbs.

   a) The storm came up suddenly. The storm came up with a loud boom of thunder.

   b) Most raced to the shed. Others just walked to the shed.

   c) At first the sky was dark. At first the streetlights were dark.

   d) The wind vibrated the trees. The wind whistled past the buildings.

   e) We huddled together under the leaky roof. We held our breath under the leaky roof.

2. Add dialogue to the story paragraph you wrote for the last activity in Writing and Revising on page 128. Be sure to review how to use quotation marks (see The Editing Desk in Unit 26).

3. Choose the correct pronoun for these sentences.

   a) Frank and _____ waited in the wings of the stage. (I, me)

   b) The buzz of the audience made _____ feel nervous. (us, we)

   c) This was the first time either Frank or _____ had been in front of so many people. (I, me)

   d) The next thing _____ knew _____ were on stage. (I, me), (us, we)

   e) Frank plugged _____ instrument into the amp. (him, his)

   f) Suddenly, the words to the song went out of _____ head. (mine, my)

   g) But after the show, someone told _____ that _____ never missed a beat. (I, me), (I, me)

   h) Well, as _____ say, the show must go on! (them, they)

4. Rewrite the following paragraph so that the pronoun references are clear. (Hint: You will have to replace some of the pronouns with proper nouns.

No matter what he says, I can't think why he wanted to treat him like that. He never meant any harm and he certainly shouldn't have taken it the way he said it. It's not as if he knew what he was talking about.

5. Look at the sentences below. Some of the verbs are used incorrectly. Rewrite these sentences with the right form of the verb. (Hint: Not all the verbs are wrong.)

   a) Every morning this year, Molly and I have risen the blinds in our classroom.

   b) Don't just set there, come and get the food!

   c) The kites rose high above the playground.

   d) I like to lay on this mat when I exercise.

   e) Her purse lay behind the desk for weeks until it was found.

   f) The moon raised high above the crystal water.

Word Play

1. Clichés are as common as the plague but not as cute as a button. Can you guess these clichés?

   a) sweet as _____

   b) solid as a _____

   c) fast as _____

   d) straight as an _____

   e) busy as a _____

   f) dead as a _____

2. Each of these formulas translates into the initials of key words in a sentence. They are tricky, but how many can you figure out? The first one has been done for you.

   a) 7D = 1 W *(seven days equals one week)*

   b) A + E + I + O + U = V

   c) S + S + M + T + W + T + F = D of the W

   d) 24 H in 1 D

   e) I B E except A C

   f) 0°C = the T at which W F

Appendix I: Word List

a lot*
absolutely
accept
account
actually
admiring
adults
advice
agree
alcohol
all right*
allowance
allowed
aloud
always*
among
amusement
anxious
appear
approximately
arcade
architect
arctic
aren't
arrival
assist
astronaut
attendance
attention
attraction
audiences
author
autograph
automatic
available
awaken
award
ballot
banquet*

barbecue
basketball
batteries
battery
because*
belief
berries
biologist
bisect
blouse
bubble
budget*
buoy
business*
butterflies'
cabinet
cafeteria
calculate
calories
canoe
capsules
captain*
career
carrot
cassette
catalogue
caught*
ceiling*
celebrating
cell phone
certainly
chalet
children's
children*
Chinese
choir*
choke
circuit
circus's

cities
citizens
classify
client
colonel
column*
commerce
commercial
committed
competition
complaint
compose
conceited
conclusion
concrete
confidence
confusion
congratulations
conquer
conqueror
consumer
content
continue
contract
conversation
convincing
cookies'
could*
coupon
courage
cousin*
crackle
creator
cruise
curious
cursor
customer
cyclist
dancing

data
debt
decision
definite
dentist
depend
deposit
depth
description
designer
desserts
diamond
didn't
difficult
digit
dilute
disagree
disappeared
disappointed
discount
disease
disobey
document
doesn't
don't
doubt
doubtful
doughnuts
download
dutiful
duty
earring
echoes
ecology
edible
education
eighth*
eighty*
either*

electrician	graduate	irregular	movie's
elevator	graph	irresistible	mysterious
employee	graveyard	it's	nature
enemies'	grief	journey's	necessary*
engineer	groan	judges'	neighbour*
enjoyment	groceries	juicy	nighttime
entrance	guest	kneel*	noises
environment	guidance	laptop	noisy
equipped	guide*	lawyer	non-fiction
escape	guilty	league*	non-profit
especially	guitar	leisure	nonsense
eventually	hadn't	length	notebook
everyone*	halves	let's	notified
exactly	hangar	lifestyle	nuclear
excellent*	hanger	limb	nuisance
except	happened*	limit	nurse
excitement	happily	lockers'	occasion
exciting	hardware	loose	occupation
exercise*	hatchback	lose	occurred
exhibit	headache	lovable	offered
experience	helicopter	machinery*	often
extinct	heroes	machinist	omitted
extraordinary	horrible	magazine	operate
fallen	horror	maintain	opinion
families	hurried	maintenance	oppose
fax	husky	major	ordered
February	icy	majority	overdue
federal	image	marriage	parallel*
feud	imagine	matches	parents'
field*	immature	mechanic	parliament
firefighter	impatient	medicine*	passengers'
flour	implied	memories	penguin
foreign	impolite	microchip	photocopy
forgive	impossible	minute	physician
forgotten	individual	mirror	pineapple
forty	industry's	misunderstand	pioneer
friends*	initials	modem	playoff
fuel	instead*	moderate	polite
garage	insurance	moisture	political
generally	interface	mortgage	politicians
geography	interfere	mosquitoes	politics
gnat	interrupt*	mountains	pore
government*	interview	mouse	potatoes

pour
prairie
prediction
prevent
probably*
proceeds
produce
profession
profit
programmer
project
qualified
quarrel
Québec
question
quietly
R.S.V.P.
raccoon
radar
realize
really
receipt
receive*
recipe
recognize
record
refer
referee*
refill
refugees
refuse
rehearse
relatives
religious
rely
rescue
reside
response
responsible
restaurant
revise
revision
rhyme

rhythm
ripped
rocky
safely
sandwich's
Saskatchewan
satisfied
Saturday*
schedule*
scholar*
schools'
scientist
scientists'
scissors
scope
scratches
scuba
semifinal
sensible
separate
separating
separation
September
shining
sigh
silently
sincere
sizzle
skeleton
skiing
society's
software
solving
sore
spaghetti
spell checker
sphere
spokesperson
spreadsheet
static
stationary
stationery
steal

steel
stomach*
strength*
students'
studied
stylish
subject
submarine's
success
successful
surely
surgeon
suspect
swiftly
syrup
teacher's
teammate
technician
teenager's
teleshopping
terribly
that's
theatre's
theory's
there's
they're
they've
thoughts*
through*
thrown
tomatoes
tongue
touch-tone
trapped
travelling
tries
turkey*
turkeys'
turtle's
twins'
umpire's
uncomfortable
unconscious

universe
university
unpopular
unreasonable
until*
unusual
uproar
usually
vacuum
valet
valuable
various
vegetables
victim's
visible*
vocation
volume
waist
ware
warranty
waste
wastebasket
watches'
wavy
we're
Wednesday
weighed
weird*
whole
windshield
witness's
women
women's
worried
worst*
wouldn't
wrecked
wrench
wrestle
wriggle
yacht
yield
you're
you've

Appendix II: Grammar Terms

Adjective: a word that tells more about a noun or pronoun (*rocky, polite, irresistible*)

Adverb: a word that tells more about a verb, adjective, or other adverb. Many adverbs end in **-ly**. (*especially, happily, silently*)

Agreement: *see pronoun–noun agreement* and *subject–verb agreement*

Capital Letters: generally used for proper nouns, the initials of people's names, the first word of a sentence, the pronoun *I*, acronyms and some abbreviations that use initials, and the names of languages, nationalities, and religions (*Chinese, A. L. Douglas, CBC*)

Colon (:): often used before a list of words or phrases (*Here is the list of ingredients: 2 eggs, 250 ml of milk, 300 g cheddar cheese, 500 ml noodles.*)

Comma (,): can be used to separate phrases, words in a list, and sentences connected by a conjunction (*Franka, Tim, and Leo live in my apartment building.*) The comma is also used with quotation marks. (*"Please pass the juice," Diane said.*)

Conjunction: a word that connects words, sentences, and phrases, such as *and, but, for, nor, or, so, yet* (*Vladimir waved, <u>but</u> the bus driver didn't see him.*)

Exclamation Mark (!): used at the end of a phrase or sentence that expresses a strong emotion (*Stop that!*)

Nouns: A noun is a word that names a person, place, or thing. There are two types of nouns, as follows:
>   ***common noun:*** the name of a place or thing that is not capitalized (*dog, book, river, apartment*)
>
>   ***proper noun:*** the name of a specific person or place. Proper nouns are usually capitalized. (*Marc Garneau, British Columbia, Riverview Drive, CN Tower*)

Participles:
>   ***past participle:*** verb tense that is usually the past-tense form of the verb. When past participles are used with the present tense of <u>to have</u>, they mean an action that starts in the past and continues into the present. (*The class <u>has competed</u> in the tournament every year.*)

present participle: verb tense that expresses an action that is happening now. Present participles are formed by combining the present tense of *to be* with the **-ing** form of a verb. (*I am taking a walk around the block.*)

Period (.): ends a sentence (*The car waited at the light.*)

Phrase: a group of words that does not express a complete thought (*going past the corner*)

Preposition: a word that shows a relationship of time, position, or direction. Prepositions connect words in a sentence to other words. (*on, at, after, to, through, within, toward*)

Pronoun–Noun Agreement: a pronoun used in a sentence must match the subject noun. (*The three players waited for their teammates to arrive.*)

Pronouns: A pronoun is a word that takes the place of, or stands for, a noun. There are several different types of pronouns. The following are just a few:

> **indefinite pronoun:** a word that takes the place of *someone* or *something* that is not definitely named. Indefinite pronouns include *everybody, anything, another, none.*
>
> **object pronoun:** often follows a preposition or a verb. Object pronouns include *me, him,* and *her*. (*Please tell me what time you have.*)
>
> **personal pronoun:** a word that stands for a person or a thing, such as *he, she, it, they, you* (*She used to attend our school.*)
>
> **subject pronoun:** often begins a sentence. When used in place of an object pronoun, a subject pronoun can alter the meaning of an idea and confuse a reader. Subject pronouns include *I, he,* and *she*. (*He didn't realize what time it was.*)

Punctuation: signals the reader to a break in a phrase or sentence. Punctuation also indicates the type of sentence. See *period, comma, question mark, exclamation mark,* and *colon*

Question Mark (?): comes at the end of a phrase or sentence that is worded in the form of a question (*What is your name?*)

Quotations:

> **direct quotation:** the exact words of a speaker; always enclosed in quotation marks (*Brianna shrieked, "Let's go!"*)
>
> **indirect quotation:** the approximate words a speaker uses; never enclosed in quotation marks (*Doug told us to close the door.*)

Sentences: A sentence is a group of words that expresses a complete thought. Every sentence needs a subject and an action.

compound sentence: two sentences connected by a conjunction (*The clock ticked away and time was running out.*)

simple sentence: has one subject and one verb (*Tom ordered pizza.*)

Subject: The subject is what a sentence is about. (*The plants in the backyard need watering.*)

compound subject: two nouns connected by a conjunction that, together, act as the subject of a sentence. A compound subject gets rid of the need to write the same sentence over again. (*Fritz jumped. Lucy jumped.* These two sentences can be rewritten as one: *Fritz and Lucy jumped.*)

Subject–Verb Agreement: the subject of a sentence must match or agree with its verb. This is especially true for the present tense. (*The car travels down the highway.* [singular]; *The cars travel down the highway.* [plural])

Tenses:

future tense: verb tense that describes an action that takes place beyond the present time. This tense is made up of *will* plus the verb. (*Who will come with me tomorrow?*)

irregular past tense: a verb tense that doesn't follow a regular pattern. The past and past-participle tenses of the verb can't be formed by just adding **-ed**. (*sing* [present tense] becomes *sang* [past tense] and *sung* [past participle])

past tense: verb tense that describes an action that happens before the present. Most fiction and non-fiction writing uses the past tense. The usual ending for a verb in the past tense is **-ed**. (*Everyone wanted to join the team.*)

present tense: verb tense that has different forms for singular and plural subjects (*The car races down the road.* [singular]; *The cars race down the road.* [plural])

Verbs: A verb tells the reader what action or state of being is happening in a sentence.

action verb: tells what the subject of the sentence is doing (*studied, wrote, hurried*)

compound verb: two verbs connected by a conjunction that, together, act as the action of a sentence. Combining verbs helps to get rid of unnecessary sentences. (*The river overflowed. The river ran down the bank.* These two sentences can be rewritten as one: *The river <u>overflowed</u> and <u>ran</u> down the bank.*)

easily confused verbs: verbs that look similar to other verbs. For some of these verbs, the past participles are not regular; that is, they don't end in **-ed**. Three common examples include *lay/lie*, *sit/set*, and *rise/raise*.

linking verb: links or connects the subject to a word that describes the subject (*Too many mosquitoes <u>are</u> outside my tent.*) The most common linking verb is *to be*. Its forms are *am, is, are, was, were, be, been,* and *being*.

regular verb patterns: the ending **-s** is added to a verb in the present tense with *he, she,* or *it*. (*Marlene buy<u>s</u> groceries in the market.*) The ending **-ed** is added to a verb to make the past tense. (*The class help<u>ed</u> the new students.*)

Appendix III: Proofreader's Marks

Mark	Meaning	Example
∧	Insert	The house ^is on fire.
℘	Delete	Rattlesnakes are very ~~very~~ dangerous.
∼	Transpose (Switch)	Raisa, Louise, and Kevin are 12, 14, and 16 years old, respectively.
⌒	Close Space	Chickens can't fly, but du⌒cks can.
#	Add Space ‿	Daniel#and I are leaving tomorrow.
≡	Capital	Planet ≡earth may be in danger.
/	Lower Case	We /Compost all our food scraps.
¶	New Paragraph	So that day ended badly. ¶ The next day...
⊙	Add Period	Liu wondered which way to go⊙
⌃	Add Comma	Bring your tent⌃a sleeping bag, and a flashlight.
⊙	Add Colon	Add these items to the list⊙bread, butter, milk, eggs.
?/	Add Question Mark	What are you going to do now?
!/	Add Exclamation Mark	Oh no, that car is on fire!
∨	Add Apostrophe	It's a beautiful day.
⌄ " / ⌄ "	Add Quotation Marks	"Close that door! he cried."